DEVIL'S ADVOCATES

I0113436

DEVIL'S ADVOCATES is a series of books devoted to exploring the classics of horror cinema. Contributors to the series come from the fields of teaching, academia, journalism and fiction, but all have one thing in common: a passion for the horror film and a desire to share it with the widest possible audience.

'The admirable Devil's Advocates series is not only essential – and fun – reading for the serious horror fan but should be set texts on any genre course.'
Dr Ian Hunter, Reader in Film Studies, De Montfort University, Leicester

'Auteur Publishing's new Devil's Advocates critiques on individual titles... offer bracingly fresh perspectives from passionate writers. The series will perfectly complement the BFI archive volumes.' **Christopher Fowler,** *Independent on Sunday*

'Devil's Advocates has proven itself more than capable of producing impassioned, intelligent analyses of genre cinema... quickly becoming the go-to guys for intelligent, easily digestible film criticism.' *Horror Talk.com*

'Auteur Publishing continue the good work of giving serious critical attention to significant horror films.' *Black Static*

facebook DevilsAdvocatesbooks

DevilsAdBooks

Also available in this series

A Girl Walks Home Alone at Night Farshid Kazemi

Black Sunday Martyn Conterio

The Blair Witch Project Peter Turner

Blood and Black Lace Roberto Curti

The Blood on Satan's Claw David Evans-Powell

Candyman Jon Towlson

Cannibal Holocaust Calum Waddell

Cape Fear Rob Daniel

Carrie Neil Mitchell

The Company of Wolves James Gracey

The Conjuring Kevin J. Wetmore Jr.

Creepshow Simon Brown

Cruising Eugenio Ercolani & Marcus Stiglegger

The Curse of Frankenstein Marcus K. Harmes

Daughters of Darkness Kat Ellinger

Dead of Night Jez Conolly & David Bates

The Descent James Marriot

The Devils Darren Arnold

Don't Look Now Jessica Gildersleeve

The Evil Dead Lloyd Haynes

The Fly Emma Westwood

Frenzy Ian Cooper

Halloween Murray Leeder

House of Usher Evert Jan van Leeuwen

In the Mouth of Madness Michael Blyth

It Follows Joshua Grimm

Ju-on The Grudge Marisa Hayes

Let the Right One In Anne Billson

M Samm Deighan

Macbeth Rebekah Owens

The Mummy Doris V. Sutherland

Nosferatu Cristina Massaccesi

Peeping Tom Kiri Bloom Walden

Possession Alison Taylor

Re-Animator Eddie Falvey

Repulsion Jeremy Carr

Saw Benjamin Poole

Scream Steven West

The Shining Laura Mee

Shivers Luke Aspell

The Silence of the Lambs Barry Forshaw

Suspiria Alexandra Heller-Nicholas

The Texas Chain Saw Massacre James Rose

The Thing Jez Conolly

Trouble Every Day Kate Robertson

Twin Peaks: Fire Walk With Me Lindsay Hallam

Witchfinder General Ian Cooper

Forthcoming

Dawn of the Dead Jon Towlson

IT: Chapters 1 & 2 Alissa Burger

Pet Sematary Shellie McMurdo

Snuff Mark McKenna

DEVIL'S ADVOCATES

THE OMEN

ADRIAN SCHOBER

auteur

Acknowledgements

I would like to acknowledge John Atkinson of Auteur/LUP for embracing the idea of a monograph on *The Omen*, and for his guidance – and patience – throughout the editorial process. I'd also like to thank his team of anonymous readers and typesetter/designer Nikki Hamlett. Also, special thanks to Hitchcock guru Ken Mogg, who read an early draft of the manuscript and provided me with much-needed reassurance.

auteur

First published in 2022 by
Auteur, an imprint of
Liverpool University Press,
4 Cambridge Street,
Liverpool
L69 7ZU

Series design: Nikki Hamlett at Cassels Design
Set by Cassels Design, Luton UK

British Library Cataloguing-in-Publication Data
A catalogue record for this book is available from the British Library

ISBN paperback: 978-1-80085-708-7
ISBN hardback: 978-1-80085-707-0
ISBN PDF: 978-1-80085-750-6

CONTENTS

Introduction 7

Chapter 1: From the Eternal Sea He Rises 27

Chapter 2: The Devil Delusion 37

Chapter 3: Until Man Fxists No More 71

Chapter 4: Satanic Anti-Hero 79

Conclusion 91

Notes 95

Bibliography 99

CONTENTS

INTRODUCTION

Directed by Richard Donner and written by David Seltzer, *The Omen* (1976) is perhaps the best in the horrific devil-child cycle of movies that came in the wake of *Rosemary's Baby* (Roman Polanksi, 1968) and *The Exorcist* (William Friedkin, 1973). Released to a highly suggestible public, *The Omen* became a major box-office hit, in no small part due to an elaborate pre-sell campaign that played and preyed on apocalyptic fears and a renewed belief in the Devil and the supernatural. It was a film that polarised critics and religious groups in equal measure. Yet almost half a century later, its place in the horror film canon is assured. While often compared to *The Exorcist* (*Rosemary's Baby*, with its Devil's spawn dénouement, is a more fitting comparison), '*The Omen* is, in fact, more functional and low-key than *The Exorcist* and is propelled more by narrative invention than by elaborate effects' (Hardy 1986: 316). It's a film that operates on different levels, is imbued with nuance, ambiguity and subtext, and is open to opposing interpretations.

Rosemary's Baby, *The Exorcist* and *The Omen* turned the Devil, along with devil-child, into a major box-office draw. This trifecta of films marked a shift from more traditional Hollywood depictions of God and the Bible (*The Robe* [Henry Koster, 1953]; *The Ten Commandments* [Cecil B. DeMille, 1956]; *The Bible: In the Beginning* [John Huston, 1966]; even *Jesus Christ Superstar* [Norman Jewison, 1973]) to alternative supernatural themes (Powers, Rothman & Rothman 1996: 131). Indeed, films about Satanism, cults and conspiracy burgeoned in the 1960s and 1970s, on both sides of the Atlantic.[1] As films overlapping with the devil-child cycle, Karen Renner (2013: 47) has argued that *Rosemary Baby*'s and *The Omen* 'formulated a sort of cinematic Urtext for the antichrist-as-child-narrative, jointly establishing its standard narrative features in the cultural imaginary'. Concomitantly, I have argued that the possessed child, as a repository of evil (as in *The Exorcist*), ought to be distinguished from the satanic child, as the incarnation of evil (Schober 2004: 19-20).

Film sociologist Andrew Tudor has diagnosed a strain of paranoia in horror films from the early 1970s, both in the American milieu and internationally. 'Of course,' he qualifies, 'there is a sense in which the horror movie itself is a paranoid form: it is founded on the supposition that we are constantly under threat from many directions. However, the seventies see an extension of that fear, partly conveyed in the typical narratives of the period, and partly conveyed through style and a tendency to dwell upon overtly horrific detail' (Tudor 1989: 66-7). *The Omen* knowingly distils this paranoia, and then some. And despite the Grand Guignol set pieces (a hanging, impaling, beheading), *The Omen* is actually quite restrained, more psychological than graphic.

More importantly, *The Omen* exploited the disorienting mood of paranoia and uncertainty in 1970s America, recovering from the twin traumas of Vietnam and Watergate, and struggling with the liberalisation of its culture and values which many saw as a sign of the nation's decline. Certainly, a confluence of religious, political and cultural factors contributed to *The Omen*'s success. It was a movie for the times, with a political subtext that helped illuminate the seeds of modern American conservatism – or its ultimate destruction. For that alone, the film is an important document of the era.

FILM SYNOPSIS

Rome, June 6, 6am. American multimillionaire and diplomat Robert Thorn (Gregory Peck) learns from the hospital chaplain, Father Spiletto (Martin Benson), that his wife Kathy (Lee Remick) has just given birth to a stillborn son in a hospital in Rome. He agrees to the clandestine adoption of a newborn boy, a substitution he keeps secret from his wife. They name the foundling Damien. A few years later Robert is appointed ambassador to Great Britain, and the family take up residence in a mansion outside of London. But at Damien's fifth birthday party, his nanny (Holly Palance) hangs herself from the ledge of the manor after an encounter with a Rottweiler. Robert is visited by a Catholic priest, Father Brennan (Patrick Troughton), at the embassy, who tells him he was present the night his son, i.e. Damien, was born. The Father is removed by a marine guard before he can elaborate. Mrs Baylock (Billie Whitelaw) mysteriously presents herself to the Thorns as a replacement for the previous nanny. When Damien accompanies his parents to an Episcopal wedding, he reacts with violent hysteria in the car. On an outing to a safari park, Kathy and Damien's car is attacked by baboons in a drive-through enclosure. That night Kathy tells Robert she has deep-seated fears and entreats him to find her a psychiatrist.

Thorn meets with Father Brennan at Bishops Park, who tells him that Damien is the son of the Devil and will kill his unborn child. He entreats Robert to go to the town of Megiddo and see a man named Bugenhagen, who can advise him on how the child must die. After their meeting, the priest is caught in a freakish storm and killed by a lightning rod that dislodges from the top of a church tower and enters his body. Kathy reveals to Robert that she is in fact pregnant, but he refuses to go along with her psychiatrist's advice to have the pregnancy terminated. Damien careens into Kathy on his tricycle as she tends to a ceiling-hung plant on the second-floor landing. At the hospital, Robert learns that Kathy has survived the fall, but, as foretold by Father Brennan, lost the baby. Meanwhile, a freelance press photographer named Jennings (David Warner), who was present at Damien's birthday party and has been watching Robert from afar, shows him photographs of the deceased nanny and priest which contain strange anomalies that seem to portend their grisly fates. At Brennan's apartment, Jennings shows him a photo he inadvertently took of himself with an imperfection that seems to suggest his own demise.

Robert and Jennings go to Rome to uncover the truth about Damien's lineage, only to discover that the old hospital was burned down five years earlier, and all birth records have been destroyed. A sister, who remembers Father Spiletto from Robert's description, directs him to a remote monastery outside of Rome. There, they encounter the fire-disfigured priest, who scrawls the name of an old Etruscan cemetery in charcoal. At the cemetery, Robert and Jennings discover the skeletal remains of a jackal, Damien's mother, as well as Robert's son, with its skull bashed in, before they are set upon by a pack of Rottweilers. At the hotel, Robert calls Kathy at the hospital in London and implores her to leave. However, Mrs Baylock pushes her out the multi-storey window. Grief-stricken, Robert travels with Jennings to the site of the ancient city of Megiddo in modern-day Israel, to meet with the exorcist-archaeologist Bugenhagen (Leo McKern) who gives Robert specific instructions on how to kill the child using ancient ceremonial daggers. But Robert, still unable to accept that Damien is the Antichrist, throws the knives away in the street. When Jennings goes to retrieve the knives, he is decapitated by a pane of glass. On his return to the mansion, Robert uses scissors to cut away Damien's hair to reveal the birthmark: 666. Mrs Baylock attacks Robert, who eventually kills her with a kitchen implement. He takes the kicking-and-screaming child into the car to a nearby church, followed by police. As he prepares to stab the child on the altar, a shot rings out from a policemen's handgun. In the coda, a military funeral reveals two caskets: Katherine's and Robert's. After the service, Damien smiles straight into camera, as he stands in between the First Lady and the President of the United States.

0.1 Harvey Stephens made an indelible impression on moviegoers as the devil-child Damien.

AVE SATANI

Unleashed in the UK on the 6th day of the 6th month 1976, *The Omen* marked the year of the Devil, at least according to 20th Century Fox's blitzkrieg publicity campaign. In feeding a seemingly insatiable appetite for Devil-inspired movies, it gained much from mounting fears about the so-called crisis in mainstream Christianity, the spread of Satanism and cults, and the end of the world. Indeed, it was as if *The Omen* was timed to exploit this 'crucible' moment in history.

In a sermon he delivered in June 1972, Pope Paul VI controversially expressed fears about the rise of the Devil's influence which he explicitly linked to the decline of the Catholic Church:

[F]rom some fissure the smoke of Satan has entered the temple of God. There is doubt, incertitude, problems, disquiet, dissatisfaction, confrontation. There is no longer trust in the Church; they [the people] trust the first profane prophet who speaks in some journal or some social movement, and they run after him and ask him if he has the formula of true life …

This state of uncertainty even holds sway in the Church. There was a belief that after the [Second Vatican] Council there would be a day of sunshine for the history of the

Church. Instead, it is the arrival of a day of clouds, of tempest, of darkness, of research, of uncertainty. We preach ecumenism but we constantly separate ourselves from others. We seek to dig abysses instead of filling them.

How has this come about? (Paul VI 2013: 436-437)

For the Pope, the answer could be found in the intervention of a hostile power whose name was the Devil.

As if confirming the Pope's worst fears, this uncertainty led to a radically different form of worship. On the 30th April 1966, Anton LaVey had founded the Church of Satan in San Francisco. Dubbed 'The Black Pope' by the press, he published *The Satanic Bible* in 1969, which became an instant bestseller. For all his notoriety, the charismatic frontman did not hold to a belief in the Devil as an actual entity, but, rather, as a symbolic representation of the rebellious, individual self. In August 1971, *Look* magazine featured him on the cover in Satanic regalia holding a skull. The story asserted that Satanism and witchcraft were on the rise in contemporary American society:

In California, police report youths are found carrying ritual bags that contain drugs, potions, animal bones and occasionally human fingers. Residents near Western mountain areas have claimed to hear eerie ceremonial chanting at night and on the following days have found skinned cats and beheaded chickens lying at abandoned campfire sites. In New York, Black Masses and voodoo rituals are openly advertised in the not-so-underground press. In a small New Jersey town, two high school members of an uncovered Satanist cult were arrested on charges of murder. And all over the country, young zealots dubbed 'Jesus freaks' say their numbers are only beginning to draw even with the practitioners of black magic. (Vachon 1971: 40-42)

A year later *TIME* ran a cover story on 'The Occult Revival: Satan Returns', which featured the image of a hooded devil worshipper with the 'Sigil of Baphomet', or goat avatar inside a pentagram (anon. a 1972). It told of how occult beliefs and practices were becoming increasingly mainstream.

This growing fascination with the occult also correlated with a larger movement within Western esoteric culture that has been christened the New Age. With roots in the 1960s counterculture, Eastern mysticism, and earlier occult and metaphysical movements, it exhibited a fascination with witchcraft or wicca, astrology, crystal healing, reincarnation, channelling, and altered states. Astrologically, New Agers believed in the coming of different eras, as read through the stars (synonymous with the so-called Age of Aquarius, immortalised in the 1967 musical *Hair*), which may be construed as a less fatalist version of dispensationalist thought (Albanese 1992: 358-9).

As first promulgated in the United States by the Anglo-Irish Bible teacher John Nelson Darby (1800-1882) in the nineteenth century, dispensationalism divided history into ages or periods, called dispensations. 'In the dispensationalist view, none of the biblical prophecies regarding the end had been fulfilled, but they soon would be. For dispensationalists, the world was growing steadily more evil, the Antichrist would soon control it, and after this period of tribulation, Jesus would return, conquer the Antichrist, and establish his kingdom for 1,000 years' (Albanese 1992: 169). In the late twentieth century, American evangelist and doomsayer (and later television host) Hal Lindsey took on Darby's mantle to popularise a premillennial dispensationalist view of the Bible. Born in 1929, Lindsey graduated with a Master of Theology from the Dallas Theological Seminary, renowned for its premillennial thought. As a preacher and missionary in the late 1960s, Lindsey associated with students for Campus Crusade for Christ (Sturm 2021: 40). In 1970 he published ('with' C.C. Carlson) the bestseller *The Late Great Planet Earth*, which outsold every other non-fiction book in the United States with the exception of the Bible (Poole 2010: 166).

In the book, Lindsey laid great stress on the Great Tribulation, a period of about seven years where there would be famine, pestilence, disasters and war. This would mark the reign of Satan in a figure called the Antichrist. The days of the Antichrist's reign would be numbered, cut short by Christ's Second Coming and the establishment of his millennial kingdom. Like many theologians, Lindsey interpreted the revived Holy Roman Empire as the formation of the European Union or Common Market, behind the scenes of which he saw the hand of the Antichrist seeking to become the ruler of Western Europe and the rest of the free world. Lindsey took America's moral, spiritual and economic decline as a harbinger of the end times:

> The United States will not hold its present position of leadership in the western world; financially, the future leader will be Western Europe. Internal political chaos

caused by student rebellions and Communist subversion will begin to erode the economy of our nation. Lack of moral principle by citizens and leaders will so weaken law and order that a state of anarchy will finally result. The military capability of the United States, though it is at present the most powerful in the world, has already become neutralized because no one has the courage to use it decisively. When the economy collapses so will the military …

As the United States loses its power, Western Europe will be forced to unite and become the standard-bearer of the western world. Look for the emergence of a "United States of Europe" composed of ten inner member nations. The Common Market is laying the groundwork for this political confederacy which will become the mightiest coalition on earth. It will stop the Communist take-over of the world and will for a short while control both Russia and Red China through the personal genius of the Antichrist who will become ruler of the European confederacy. (Lindsey & Carlson 1971: 184-185)

Stoking Protestant fears of a Roman Catholic plot, Lindsey further called on readers to look out for the papacy seeking to exert a greater influence on world politics (Lindsey & Carlson 1971: 185).

Prior to the release of *The Omen*, the when and how of the apocalypse was much debated. The Pennsylvania-founded Jehovah's Witnesses had pinpointed 1975 as the probable year for the end times, or Armageddon, as revealed in the Book of Revelation to the apostle John; the failure of this prediction led to a sharp drop in the denomination's membership. As faith in mainstream Protestant churches declined in the United Sates, such premillennial apocalyptic fears found particular urgency in the Pentecostalist and Fundamentalist movements, and in the so-called Evangelical Resurgence of the 1970s. The American publication *Newsweek* proclaimed 1976 'The Year of the Evangelical' (Boyer 2008: 29), while *Christianity Today* observed: 'Evangelicals suddenly find themselves number one on the North American religious scene. Thanks to media visibility, they are seizing the public imagination. There is unprecedented interest in many aspects of the evangelical outlook' (Kucharsky 1976: 13). At its forefront was American fire-and-brimstone preacher Billy Graham, who also subscribed to a belief in the end times.

Which is to say that *The Omen*, for all its Catholic trappings, is more Protestant and even Evangelical in its outlook and eschatology. As W. Scott Poole (2010: 165) points out in *Satan in America: The Devil We Know*: 'If *Rosemary's Baby* and *The Exorcist* reflected, and even helped to shape, a new evangelical fascination with the devil's influence, *The Omen* drew directly on this fascination for its plot and source material.' This supplied David Seltzer with 'the basic story arc' for the movie (Poole 2010: 165), leading to an ex-post facto trilogy, followed by *Damien: Omen II* (Don Taylor, 1978) and *The Final Conflict* (Graham Baker, 1981). (We may easily ignore the late-entry, made-for-TV *Omen IV: The Awakening* [1991, Jorge Montesti and Dominique Othenin-Girard].)

Interestingly, *The Omen* seems to have anticipated, by several years, the Satanic panic that swept the United States in the 1980s. This involved baseless claims about cults and ritual abuse, often overlapping with a new psychiatric diagnosis: recovered memory syndrome. The hysteria also spread to other countries such as Great Britain, despite a lack of evidence. As Elaine Showalter documents in *Hysteries: Hysterical Pandemics and Modern Culture* (1997: 174): 'Alleged victims of satanic cults describe conspiracies by huge, intergenerational, secretive criminal organizations that maintain total control over their members and victims; [where] leaders would avoid detection by living in disguise as normal members of the community.' The cultural impact of films like *Rosemary's Baby* and *The Omen* may have even contributed to the emergence of this panic.

PARANOIA

In having the story of the Antichrist's ascension in England end with his implied residency in the White House, *The Omen* goes right to the fear of corruption and conspiracy in American government. This linking of Satan with the nation's politics goes back to colonial and revolutionary times; a lithograph has Thomas Jefferson 'kneeling before the altar of the French Revolution, an altar supported by none other than Satan himself' (Poole 2010: 24). Jefferson was even aligned with the Antichrist, as would be later presidents such as John F. Kennedy, Richard Nixon, Barack Obama, and Donald Trump. *The Omen* makes explicit the link between Satan and politics, and after revelations about the Pentagon Papers, Watergate and other agency cover-ups, it was perhaps not too much of a leap to think that there might be Satanic forces at work in the White House;

indeed, that Richard Nixon, the 37th President of the United States and a Republican to boot, might be Satan himself. In the June 1994 edition of *Rolling Stone*, Hunter S. Thompson eulogised Nixon as 'an evil man – evil in a way that only those who believe in the physical reality of the Devil can understand it. He was utterly without ethics or morals or any bedrock of decency.'

It was as if the United States, its institutions inherently corrupt and beyond salvation, had lost its presumption of innocence, bound up with the twin fictions of Manifest Destiny and American exceptionalism. And as historians Kevin M. Kruse and Julian E. Zelizer (2019: 9) observe in their thought-provoking *Fault Lines: A History of the United States Since 1974*, 'in the wake of Vietnam and Watergate, the soundness of "the establishment" suddenly seemed in doubt. President Lyndon Johnson had left the White House with his credibility shattered by the war abroad, and then President Richard Nixon resigned in disgrace over scandal at home. In the aftermath, Americans wondered if the entire nation was following its presidents to ruin.' This sense of anomie and despair was further exacerbated by unelected successor Gerald Ford's pardoning of Nixon in September 1974. As further evidence of *The Omen*'s perfect timing, the film's release in 1976 was also the year of the American bicentennial celebrations, when the nation was reflecting on its past glories as well as recent traumas. While President Ford sought to unite the politically fractured nation in these celebrations, trust in government institutions plunged from an all-time high of 80 per cent in 1966 to around 25 per cent in 1981 (Kruse & Zelizer 2019: 34).

The toxic lack of trust in government institutions manifested itself as paranoia, fomented in the 1960s with conspiracy theories about the 1963 assassination of President John F. Kennedy, mounting doubts over the findings of the Warren Report, and the slaying of Kennedy's brother Robert later in the decade. This suspicion, insecurity and fear reached new intensity in the 1970s, prompting British journalist Francis Wheen to label these years the Golden Age of Paranoia, 'a pungent *mélange* of apocalyptic dread and conspiratorial fever' (Wheen 2007: 9). It not only expressed itself in the increasingly 'paranoid style' of Nixon's administration, plagued with cover-ups and scandals, but also in hoax theories about the Apollo moon landings, the apocalyptic predictions of mainstream and fringe religions, doomsday cults such as Reverend Jim Jones's Peoples Temple, and an acute sense of doom regarding environmental damage and the impact of over-population.

To come to the point, the keynote of *The Omen* is a 1970s style of paranoia and conspiracy, viewed through an American prism. As wedded to a Satanic plot, an important precedent here is *Rosemary's Baby*, which similarly plays into a 1960s style of paranoia and conspiracy, containing references to the Catholic Kennedys and a clandestine coven of Satanists (Newton 2020: 78). In the 1970s, a new generation of American left-wing filmmakers captured the national mood. In *A Cinema of Loneliness*, Robert Kolker (2011: 275) chronicles the films that 'were a conduit for the shudder that went through the culture and its dominant ideologies during the sixties and seventies', in which 'images and narratives of despair and impotence alternated or were combined with violent outbursts against the self and others'. These films spoke of paranoia and loss: *The Conversation* (Francis Ford Coppola, 1974); Alan J. Pakula's 'paranoid trilogy', *Klute* (1971), *The Parallax View* (1974) and *All the President's Men* (1976); *Three Days of the Condor* (Sydney Pollack, 1975); *Marathon Man* (John Schlesinger, 1976); and *Invasion of the Body Snatchers* (Philip Kaufman, 1978). 'Common to all paranoid texts of the period,' argues Paul Cobley (2002: 75) 'is a concern with the deceptiveness of appearances, the way that the familiar becomes threatening. Yet, what is crucial about the paranoid text of the seventies is that it is the site of a complex and contradictory political struggle. Nixonian and anti-Nixonian paranoia enjoyed a symbiotic relationship.' *The Omen* ought to be included among this corpus of paranoid texts. In its chronicling of the devil-child's rise from the House of Thorn into the White House, the film is likewise the site of a political struggle, both Nixonian and anti-Nixonian in its implications.

These different aspects of paranoia – stemming from mainstream, fringe and alternative religion, politics and government, intergenerational strife, child rearing – are unpacked over the course of this book. As I hope to show, *The Omen* not only has significance as a horror film-cum-mystery-suspense thriller (with ambiguous layers and meanings), but also as a quasi religio-political polemic, assuming one is able to take it all seriously. However, illuminating the film's subtext here is fraught with difficulty, complicated by an ending that came almost as an afterthought. Not only would this birth a trilogy, but it would have far-reaching implications for the meanings we take away from the movie. Was *The Omen* a revolutionary text espousing an end-of-the-world nihilism, as noted critic Robin Wood took it? Or a warning to conservatives to take action soon or else all hell will break loose? In this book, I argue that the film is ideologically conflicted, pitched somewhere between radical, left-wing ideas and the secular and religious right.

I argue that the paranoia-driven nature of the narrative is much more equivocal than has been hitherto acknowledged, pivoting as it does on the construction of the devil-child. While the majority of critics (and viewers) took it as a given that Damien is the son of the Devil and must be ritually slain, Richard Donner's intention was much more subtle: to make 'two pictures' with opposing interpretations, in which the supernatural reality coexists with an alternative, that is, rational explanation. In this way, the ambassador, according to Donner, is a victim of circumstance. For the most part, this Devil's Advocates entry treats *The Omen* on its own terms, before it spawned two theatrical sequels (with diminishing box-office returns), a made-for-television movie, an unnecessary 2006 remake (which recycles Seltzer's script almost verbatim) and short-lived television series. However, I believe it would be remiss not to give some attention to the larger trajectory of Damien's journey in the two sequels that form the trilogy proper.

BACKGROUND

The story of how *The Omen* got made isn't particularly auspicious. Indeed, it came close to not being made at all. In 1974, advertising executive – and born-again Christian – Robert Munger conceived the idea of the Antichrist reborn as an infant, thus providing the basic premise for the story. (Munger would serve as the film's religious adviser.) He communicated his idea to friend and producer Harvey Bernhard, who was so enthralled that he wrote an outline. Bernhard's unremarkable credits up to that point included television documentaries and the Blaxploitation pictures *The Mack* (Michael Campus, 1973) and *Thomasine & Bushrod* (Gordon Parks Jr., 1974). To flesh this out into script form, he approached up-and-coming writer David Seltzer, who had three feature film credits to his name (as well as uncredited input on *Willy Wonka and the Chocolate Factory* [Mel Stuart, 1971]). After initially turning Bernhard down, Seltzer reconsidered out of financial necessity, reflecting: 'I did not want to do a horror film, and then I realised that I had never read the Bible, so this would be an opportunity to dive into the Bible and look for a story' (*The Omen Legacy*, 2001). Ironically, the Jewish Seltzer never took the ideas and premise seriously. He delivered the screenplay in a year, and it was then shopped around to the major studios.

0.2 Director Richard Donner at the National Film Society convention, May 1979. Photo: Alan Light. (Creative Commons license)

Despite the tried-and-tested market for this kind of fare, the screenplay proved a hard sell. It was eventually optioned by Warner Bros. under the title *The Antichrist*, but not after the other studios had passed on it. Warners, however, allowed its interest in the property to lapse as it channelled its energies into a sequel to *The Exorcist*. (Directed by John Boorman and released in 1977, *Exorcist II: The Heretic* proved a critical and commercial debacle.) As its option was about to expire, the screenplay landed on the desk of a director eager to prove himself in Hollywood. Born in the Bronx to Jewish parents in 1930, the photogenic Richard Donald Schwartzberg – aka Richard Donner – initially harboured ambitions to be an actor. For a while, he was a member of the Greenwich Village Theatre. But it was formerly blacklisted director Martin Ritt who suggested he try directing and Donner became Ritt's assistant. And like so many other directors who emerged in the 1960s and 1970s – John Frankenheimer, Franklin J. Schaffner, William Friedkin, Steven Spielberg, Ridley Scott – he earned his apprenticeship in television. He quickly graduated from directing commercials to episodes of *Wanted: Dead or Alive*, *The Twilight Zone*, *The Fugitive*, *The Man from U.N.C.L.E* and *Kojak*, as well as the topical television film, *Sarah T. Portrait of a Teenage Alcoholic* (1975), starring a post-*Exorcist* Linda Blair. He was, notes biographer James Christie (2010: 95), neither Old Hollywood nor New Hollywood, but 'somewhere in between'.[2] By the time he was considering *The Omen/The Antichrist* as his next project, Donner had three not-so-distinguished features on his CV: the aviation drama *X-15* (1961), and two films made in England, the crime comedy *Salt and Pepper* (1968) and quirky romantic-comedy *Twinky* (1969), starring Charles Bronson as a writer of erotic novels in a tempestuous relationship with an English schoolgirl. *The Omen* was to be Donner's breakout movie.

To help get the picture made, Donner approached his former agent Alan Ladd Jr., then head of production at 20th Century Fox. The studio had previously passed on the option, but Ladd now agreed that the screenplay had potential. He also agreed that the overt Satanic imagery had to be jettisoned before it could be greenlit. As Donner recalled in the 2001 documentary *The Omen Legacy*: '[Ladd] said, "There are a lot of very obvious things [in the script]," and I said, "That's what we eliminate." It had cloven hoofs, devil gods, it had covens, it was very heavy-handed. And we wanted to make it like a coincidence in somebody's life. He said, 'If you can do that, it's sold.'" Seltzer revised his script along these lines to make the actions and events seem more subtle and coincidental. Almost certainly to avoid confusion with the Italian horror film *The Antichrist* (Alberto De Martino, 1974), a shameless rip-off of *The Exorcist*, it was retitled *The Birthmark*.

The production was approved on a modest budget of $2.8 million and an 11-week shooting schedule, with location work in London, Rome and Jerusalem. British cinematographer Gil Taylor, whose previous credits included *A Hard Day's Night* (Richard Lester, 1964), *Dr Strangelove, or How I Learned to Stop Worrying and Love the Bomb* (Stanley Kubrick, 1964) and *Frenzy* (Alfred Hitchcock, 1972), was responsible for the alternately dark, baroque, and muted palette; visually, aesthetically, he imbued the film with an ambience of darkness. Principal photography began in October 1975 and ended in January 1976. Additional photography took place at Shepperton Studios, Surrey, England. While filming inside a London hospital, the title was changed from *The Birthmark* to *The Omen*, after the unanticipated negative reaction from medical staff. And as with *The Exorcist*, the production was rife with rumours of a curse, duly exploited by Fox's public relations department.

0.3 Gregory Peck as the conflicted statesman, Robert Thorn.

Gregory Peck was cast in the lead role of Robert Thorn, after it was turned down by fellow Hollywood veterans Charlton Heston and William Holden (who would appear as Robert's brother Richard in *Damien: Omen II*). Peck, who was born in California in 1916, began his career at the top, becoming one of the most popular Hollywood actors from the 1940s to the early 1960s. He won a Best Actor Academy Award for his portrayal of an idealistic, liberal lawyer from the American South in *To Kill a Mockingbird* (Robert Mulligan, 1962). While obituaries for the actor called attention to his sober, earnest masculinity and his preference for roles exhibiting 'moral fiber' (Grimes 2003), detractors took aim at the moral one-dimensionality of his persona. A proud liberal, Peck was also president of the Academy of Motion Picture Arts and Sciences from 1967 to 1970, during which he pushed for more diverse and youthful representation in its membership. By the early 1970s, after the underperformance of his recent movies, he was no longer a box-office draw and in semi-retirement. Eager to find solace in work following the suicide of his son, Peck took a chance on *The Omen*, instantly lending the production prestige and legitimacy. Donner would push Peck's persona to the limit to reveal cracks in his masculinity, but not without resistance by the actor, eliciting arguably one of his finest performances, conveying real nuance and undercurrents of guilt and brooding. Due to the film's success, Peck was introduced to a younger audience and his career experienced something of a revival.

With Peck in place, it was easy to get Lee Remick on board as his emotionally brittle wife Katherine. From a later era than Peck, Remick was born in Boston in 1935 and studied acting at the Actors Studio. She acted in roles that showcased a frank sexuality: including as an alleged rape victim in *Anatomy of a Murder* (Otto Preminger, 1959), a pathetic alcoholic in *Days of Wines and Roses* (Blake Edwards, 1962), for which she earned an Academy Award nomination for Best Actress, and Frank Sinatra's nymphomaniac wife in *The Detective* (Gordon Douglas, 1968). By the time she signed on to *The Omen* her star was on the wane. She leapt at the chance to work with Peck.

Cherubic unknown Harvey Spencer Stephens, born and bred in England, was a last-minute replacement for the pivotal role of Damien, after the original choice was withdrawn by his father. Stephens got the part only after he was egged on by Donner to attack him. His blond hair was dyed dark brown for the part. (Stephens would have bit parts in only two other films, including as a tabloid reporter in the pointless 2006 *Omen*

0.4 Lee Remick as Robert's wife Kathy, visibly unravelling in The Omen.

remake.) The rest of the cast was filled out by English character actors, including: the scene-stealing Patrick Troughton (best known as the second doctor on the British sci-fi series *Doctor Who*) as Father Brennan; David Warner (who had an uncredited role as the village idiot in Sam Peckinpah's 1971 essay on violence, *Straw Dogs*) as Keith Jennings; Billie Whitelaw (then best known for her collaborations with Irish playwright Samuel Beckett) as Mrs Baylock; and Martin Benson as Father Spiletto. Australian Leo McKern also has a memorable (but uncredited) role as Antichrist authority Carl Bugenhagen.

The Omen was edited by Stuart Baird, whose only film credits up that point were three films by Ken Russell (*The Devils*, 1971, as assistant editor; *Tommy*, 1975; *Lisztomania*, 1975). He brought to it an unerring sense of rhythm, using fast and slow editing, cross-cutting, overlapping techniques, and slow motion.

Jerry Goldsmith was commissioned to write the unique and unforgettable score. Born to Romanian Jewish parents in 1929, Goldsmith was inspired to write film music after watching Alfred Hitchcock's *Spellbound* (1945) with its mesmeric score by Miklós Rózsa. He learned something about composition and orchestration from Rózsa at the University of Southern California, before dropping out of his course to enrol in the more hands-on music program at Los Angeles City College. In addition to Rózsa, he was influenced by Igor Stravinsky, Béla Bartók, Bernard Herrmann, and Aaron Copland. By the time Goldsmith was commissioned to write the score for *The Omen*, the prolific film composer had already garnered several Academy Award nominations, including for *The Sand Pebbles* (Robert Wise, 1966), *Planet of the Apes* (Franklin J. Schaffner, 1968), *Patton* (Franklin J. Schaffner, 1969), and *Chinatown* (Roman Polanksi, 1974). At Donner's request,

Alan Ladd Jr. made a special allowance in the film's modest budget to secure his services for *The Omen*. And as Donner effusively acknowledged, the score, which would win its composer a highly deserved Academy Award, contributed immeasurably to the film's impact and success. Like Herrmann's shrieking violins in *Psycho* (Alfred Hitchcock, 1960) or John Williams' primeval ostinato in *Jaws* (Steven Spielberg, 1975), the terrifying use of Gregorian chants is an extra voice in the film. The chilling 'Ave Satani' theme, which the Academy also nominated for Best Original Song, was conceived as a liturgical inversion of 'Ave Maria', the Latin Mass reimagined as a Black Mass. In the theme, we can discern unmistakable echoes of German composer Carl Orff's well-known 'O Fortuna' from the 1937 cantata *Carmina Burana*. As we shall see, Goldsmith's extra-diegetic music goes beyond the visuals to inform — structure, frame — how we read certain scenes and moments not carried by the visuals alone, adding a further 'demonological' layer of significance to Damien's otherwise realistic construction. Interpreted differently, the score may also be acting as *counterpoint* to the visuals.

MARKETING AND RECEPTION

As a prestige production with big names, *The Omen* was given a pre-release build-up and wide release that drew on the cross-promotion and saturation methods learned from the first summer blockbuster, *Jaws*. For this purpose, Fox hired a New York advertising agency, allocating $2.8 million (equivalent to the film's budget) to the publicity campaign, which, along with the usual theatrical trailers, radio and TV spots, sneak previews and extra press screenings, consisted of billboards on highways, subways and buses, print ads, and placards in bookstores (with a life-sized cut-out of Damien) counting down the days to the end of the world or, rather, the film's release. 'Remember … you have been warned', portended one of the hundreds of teaser ads, accompanied by an image of Damien with the stylised reflection of a jackal (and three sixes nestled inside the 'O' of the title), watched over by his worried, ersatz parents (Peck and Remick). Other variations on the tagline included: 'It is a warning foretold for thousands of years. It is our final warning. It is *The Omen*' and 'If something frightening happens to you today, think about it. It may be *The Omen*.' In England and London in particular (which forms a good part of the film's backdrop), it was the subject of a $500,000 campaign in sneak previews (anon. b 1976: 29).

Because it was based on an original screenplay, there was no book (unlike *Rosemary's Baby*, *The Exorcist* or *Jaws*) to generate pre-sell interest. David Seltzer happily filled the gap, and, written during production, the tie-in novelisation was published by Signet in the US and Futura in the UK. Coming out just weeks before the film, *Boxoffice* reported that the initial Signet print run of 875,000 sold out in three weeks, and more copies were rushed into bookstores (anon. c 1976: 12). It would eventually sell over six million copies, and it may be 'the top-selling novelization of all time' (Guariento 2019: 70). '[It's] enduring success,' notes S.M. Guariento (2019: 70), 'has blurred the nature of its generation, resulting in the widespread conception – encouraged, to some extent, by publishers – that the novel preceded the film.' The novelisation, which seems to be drawing from an earlier iteration of the screenplay, differs in names and character conception (adding fascinating back-story) and plot construction. In the early Signet edition, Robert Thorn is called Jeremy Thorn, renamed in the movie because of the unintentional echoes with disgraced British MP Jeremy Thorpe, making headlines at the time. Together with the ad campaign, the novelisation succeeded in generating hype for the upcoming Fox release. Donner was adamant that it be marketed as a mystery-suspense thriller rather than a horror film. The theatrical trailer hence presents *The Omen* as a 'film of psychological suspense' which plays up the ambiguity of events in the storyline: 'Was it an accident? Was it murder? Was it coincidence? Or was it an Omen?'

Following sneak previews in US cities on June 6, 1976, *The Omen* was released into over 500 theatres nationwide with an 'R' for Restricted rating on June 25. The box-office returns exceeded the expectations of both Bernhard and Alan Ladd Jr., which immediately led to an announcement for three theatrical sequels (only two came to be made) (anon. b 1976: 3). 'In the first three days alone,' it was reported, 'it took more than $4 million [in US dollars], breaking every existing record in Fox's forty-nine year history. A mere fifty-eight days later, it had nudged over the $40 million mark …' (Castell 1976: 102). According to Box Office Mojo, *The Omen* grossed $60.9 million (around $280 million today, if adjusted for inflation, making it one of the most profitable horror films ever made). In North America, it became the sixth highest-grossing film of 1976 (behind *All the President's Men*, whose treatment of the Watergate scandal was the unspoken 'other' of *The Omen*) with $28.5 million in US rentals (Finler 2003: 360-1). As well as propelling its former TV turned film director into the high stakes – Donner's next project was the much-hyped *Superman: The Movie* (1978) for Warners – it rescued the fiscally-troubled Fox, helping to finance another record-breaking film, *Star Wars* (George Lucas, 1977; retitled *Star Wars IV: A New Hope*).

While capturing the imagination of audiences in America and abroad, critics were divided over the merits of *The Omen*. Many considered it a stylish and well-crafted horror film, even with the inevitable comparisons with *The Exorcist*. Despite off-putting aspects – namely, grisly deaths – the *Los Angeles Times* called it 'an absolutely riveting, thoroughly scary experience, a triumph of sleek craftsmanship that will inevitably but not necessarily unfavourably be compared to *The Exorcist*' (Thomas 1976: G1). Richard Schickel (1976: 46), writing for *TIME*, agreed: 'Farfetched in subject matter, but not far out in its handling of it, *The Omen* speaks well of the Devil – and of the virtues of solid commercial craftsmanship.' *Variety* wrote: 'Richard Donner's direction is taut. Performances and players all are strong, and the violence, utilized with discretion and economy, is properly motivated' (Murf. 1976: 23). The noted film critic and academic Robin Wood (1976: 12) found *The Omen* nothing short of 'astonishing, while not valuing it highly as a work of art', seeing it as less 'serious' than *The Exorcist*. Wood sought to unpack the nihilistic implications of its 'twist' ending, using *The Texas Chainsaw Massacre* (Tobe Hooper, 1974) as a point of comparison. Apropos of *The Exorcist* comparison, *Films in Review* thought '*The Omen* takes the laurels, as it is infinitely more subtle in its horror, and, additionally, infinitely more elegant as regards visual detail' (Dean 1976: 440). The *Independent Film Journal* called it a 'handsomely mounted and chillingly effective excursion through a series of nightmarish incidents' (Perchaluk 1976: 13).

However, other critics were scathing in their dismissal of the film. The *Washington Post* thought it 'just about as "scary" as *The Exorcist*, and just about as silly' (Shales 1976: C1). A backhanded compliment came from the *New York Times*: 'A member of the *Exorcist* family, it is a dreadfully silly film, which is not to say that it is totally bad. Its horrors are not horrible, its terrors are not terrifying, its violence is ludicrous – which may be an advantage – but it does move along' (Eder 1976: 12). *Saturday Review's* Judith Crist (1976: 43) was to the point: '*The Exorcist* or even *Rosemary's Baby* it isn't.' 'A matter-of-fact exercise in Satanic blood and thunder, both less grandiloquently and less pretentiously put together than *The Exorcist*' (Combs 1976: 170), wrote *Monthly Film Bulletin*. *Cinefantastique* usually more sympathetic to such genre offerings, reviewed the film cynically as a 'slick, fairly well-made piece of commercialism, aimed at producing the kind of squeamishness that made *Rosemary's Baby* and *The Exorcist* so popular' (Counts 1976: 27).

Critics targeted the serious tone of the film, a hallmark of American horror films of the 1970s. Thus, *Chicago-Sun Times'* Roger Ebert (1976: 63): 'What Jesus was to the 1950s movie epic, the devil is to the 1970s, and so all of this material is approached with the greatest solemnity, not only in the performances but also in the photography, the music and very looks on people's faces.' He gave the film two-and-a-half stars out of four (the 'thumbs down'). But Crist (1976: 43) was the most unsparing here: 'Donner … conducts the incredible doings with a straight face, and the actors respond in kind. The resulting idiocy offers more laughs than the average comedy.'

It is true to say that there is a 'high seriousness' to *The Omen* that seems to cancel out knowingness, irony, Brechtian distance, or levity – true at least until the final frames, analysed in Chapter 3. This receives particular force in the demeanour of Gregory Peck as the venerable American ambassador under duress; he is the epitome of gravitas. It also attests to the professionalism of the actor who admitted he didn't 'take the Satanic element very seriously' (Shay 1976: 42). Before the postmodern, self-reflexive turn in horror films, it's this aspect of *The Omen* that gives it its conviction, and provides the necessary suspension of disbelief, even while we sense the presence of the film's director with his tongue in his cheek. We may note how the makers of the less carefully crafted sequels sought to preserve this tone, courting similar criticisms.

The response from the religious community was predictably split. On the one hand, Donner and Bernhard, amazingly, received special awards from the California Graduate School of Theology (established in 1969) for 'daringly taking a step into a new type of dramatization of a biblical doctrine – the existence of the Antichrist and the Mark of the Beast' (anon. d 1976: 6). The National Council of Churches (an ecumenical organisation made up of Protestant, Anglican, Orthodox and other likeminded churches, excluding the Catholic Church) had only praise for *The Omen*, seeing it as a stimulus for reading the Bible. On the other hand, *Christianity Today*'s reviewer felt that 'the producers have made a pretty muddle of prophecy, so do not imagine that you will need the theologians to help you sort it out: it is pre-Sunday-school stuff' (Howard 1976: 1121). The National

Catholic Office for Motion Pictures expressed disapproval, awarding *The Omen* a 'B' for 'partly objectionable', one short of a C for 'condemned', for fostering misconceptions about Biblical prophecy (anon. e 1976: 5). This is of course not surprising, given that the film also plays into the hands of conspiracy theorists of a plot by the Catholic order, as emissaries of Satan, to take over the free world. However, for reasons touched on earlier, *The Omen* resonated with fundamentalist, evangelical and born-again movements that would come together into the so-called religious Right. Whether *The Omen* is pro- or anti-establishment is, as we shall discover, an open question.

CHAPTER 1: FROM THE ETERNAL SEA HE RISES

When the Jews return to Zion
And a comet rips the sky
And the Holy Roman Empire rises
Then you and I must die
From the eternal sea he rises
Creating armies on either shore
Turning man against his brother
'Til man exists no more
– Father Brennan in *The Omen* (1976)

When moviegoers saw *The Omen* for the first time in the summer of 1976, many were so taken by its chilling Biblical forecast that they took the above rhyme as quoted directly from the Good Book itself. In drawing on the Bible as a literary source for his treatment, in particular the Book of Revelation, Seltzer muses in the feature-length documentary *The Omen Legacy* (2001): 'There is a lot be mined in the Bible, and as a book there is a reason that it is a bestseller. It's fascinated people since the time it was written. It's inspiring, it's scary, it's consoling, and it's forewarning.' On the film's beguiling piece of religious doggerel, *pastiche* is the right word, says Seltzer: 'I made up the rhyme but I did not make up the prediction of these events. I went in every possible way I could with the Biblical symbolism, from the Book of Revelations [sic].' As well as consulting various translations of Revelation, he looked at interpretive texts by theological scholars. Hal Lindsey's *The Late Great Planet Earth* seems a likely source, including speculations about America's so-called decline, European unification, Vatican conspiracy theory, the creation of a modern Jewish state, and other world events. Seltzer's verse predictions further riff on the collection of prophecies (written in quatrains) by sixteenth-century French astrologer and 'seer' Nostradamus.

The Omen begins in Rome, the seat of Roman Catholic power, home of the Vatican and chief residence of popes since medieval times. In 1929, Vatican City was founded as an independent sovereign state, with its own laws and authority. When we meet Robert Thorn he is in the back seat of a limousine, appearing solemn as he is chauffeured through the city's streets in the early hours – or, as the title states exactly, 'Rome June 6th – 6am'. An asynchronous voice-over, belonging to Father Spiletto laments: 'The child is dead. He breathed for a moment, then he breathed no more. The child is dead. Dead. The child is dead …' Donner then shoots the tête-à-tête between statesman and Italian priest through a row of balusters overlooking the anteroom of the Catholic hospital, as Robert comes to terms with the news that his son has just died on delivery. It's as if we are flies on the wall, overhearing a secret conversation – and, in due course, a plot. The manner of framing also suggests how this is unfolding under Satan's watchful eye.

1.1 Robert and Father Spiletto (Martin Benson) through the balusters.

When Spiletto hesitantly suggests they adopt a child, Robert intimates that Kathy wanted her own. But he reconsiders, and thereby enters into a conspiracy, one in which his stillborn will be substituted for a newborn, born in the exact same moment his son has died. The foundling, the Father assures the diplomat, has no relatives; its mother has died in childbirth. They make an implicit vow of secrecy – not even his wife will be aware of the deception. 'On this night, Mr Thorn,' the priest pronounces, 'God has given you a son.' But his words will carry a terrible irony.

For unbeknownst to us, Father Spiletto, and his accomplice Father Brennan – the Irish priest who later repents and tries to warn Robert of the true identity of the 'son' he has brought into his home – are in fact renegade priests, apostates of Satan. They make the not-so-innocent Robert a party to a much larger conspiracy to orchestrate the Antichrist's return on Earth. Nikolas Schreck (2001: 181) is for the most part right that 'Satan, as perceived in *The Omen*, has no other meaning than as a counterpart to Christianity, a faith piously affirmed in the picture's solemn tone. As such, the film has little to say about Satanism or black magic as a phenomenon in its own right, and is purely an expression of Biblical orthodoxy.'Yet as critic Penelope Gilliatt (1978: 86) picked up on at the time, horror films like *The Omen* and *Damien: Omen II* 'play on a vulgar streak of anti-popery that lingers in Anglo-Saxon countries. Perhaps the fact that Catholicism now yields the most potent idea of the Devil has led filmmakers to make hay with this prejudice.' Roman Catholicism, as the go-to religion of Hollywood horror, informs such movies as *Rosemary's Baby, The Exorcist, The Amityville Horror* (Stuart Rosenberg, 1979), *Amityville II: The Possession* (Damiano Damiani, 1982) and, latterly, *Stigmata* (Rupert Wainwright, 1999).

In the case of *The Omen*, it makes hay with a prejudice of a Roman Catholic conspiracy to gain control and enforce Satan's will over nations under the guise of Christianity, which finds its antisemitic counterpart in a worldwide Jewish conspiracy. Anti-Catholic sentiment thrived in the Puritan New England colonies of the United States. After a period of relative tolerance, this ill-feeling grew in the nineteenth century with the arrival of Roman Catholic, including Irish immigrants to the country (Alabanese 1992: 505-506). In the early twentieth century the revived Ku Klux Klan made Catholics, along with blacks and Jews, their national enemies, inscribed in classic projective fashion as 'others'. And so, 'Satan cloaked in the red robes of the Catholic Church became a permanent part of Protestant America's conception of demonic evil. Reborn in the 1920s, fear of Satan's work through Catholicism would find new life in a renewed nativism. A supposed connection between the Catholic Church and the work of the Antichrist made end-time speculation an especially virulent discourse' (Poole 2009: 72). Thus, when Democrat Al Smith was defeated in the presidential primaries of 1928, the Protestant majority feared his Catholic faith would make him a puppet of the Pope in Rome. It was not until 1960 that the nation was prepared to elect its first Catholic president in Democrat John Fitzgerald Kennedy, but not, significantly, without controversy. And we had to wait nearly 60 years for a second Catholic president in Joe Biden – another Democrat – who has placed his faith more front and centre.

'Jack', along with wife Jackie, brought a fashionable face to American Catholicism. And Kennedy seemed to embody the homegrown ideal that one's religious affiliation did not matter to election to its highest office. However, his election campaign sparked debates about Catholicism and politics in American society. In the literal demonisation of

Kennedy and his religion during the campaign, 'Mass-produced pamphlets, from extreme anti-Catholic organizations, recapitulated the centuries-old belief that the Roman Catholic pope ruled as a living antichrist' (Carty 2004: 3). Kennedy was rumoured by some right-wing elements to be part of a popish plot, if not the Antichrist himself; he was said to have received 666 votes at the 1956 Democratic Convention.

Such irrational fears find expression in the celebrated dream sequence of *Rosemary's Baby*, where hopeful mother Rosemary Woodhouse (Mia Farrow) imagines she is on a yacht with JFK in navy uniform, who bars her close friend Hutch (Maurice Evans) from coming on board, saying, 'Catholics only. I wish we weren't bound by these prejudices, but unfortunately ….' She later 'imagines' herself naked on the bed, surrounded by naked members of a coven, including next-door neighbours Roman (Ralph Bellamy) and Minnie Castavet (Ruth Roman), as well as her scheming actor husband Guy (John Cassavetes), as they subject her to Satanic ritual abuse. Before she is raped by a cloven-hoofed figure, a glamorous Jackie sympathises, 'I'm sorry to hear you haven't been feeling well', before advising, 'You better have your legs tied down, in case of convulsions.' The Pope also appears in the dream carrying a suitcase, expressing his concern for Rosemary's health, granting his forgiveness, and proffering his Piscatory Ring for her to kiss. Roman Catholicism, as Tony Williams (2014: 100) argues, is depicted 'as exclusive as satanism with its particular rites. The dream sequence implicitly suggests the real reasons behind JFK's surprising 1960 electoral victory.' The Catholic, guilt-ridden Rosemary is tricked into bearing the son of the Devil. Despite critics' lazy comparisons with *The Exorcist*, Don Shay (1976: 46) was closer to the truth that 'if Rosemary been separated from her child as planned all along by the coven, *The Omen* could have almost been a sequel.'

As a multi-millionaire, diplomat and presidential hopeful, it has to be significant that Thorn – like JFK – is Catholic (at least implicitly) and not Protestant. The novelisation gives more background on this point: 'The Thorns were both of Catholic parentage, but neither of them were religious. Kathy was given to occasional prayer and visits to Church on Christmas and Easter, but more out of superstition and sentiment than a belief in Catholic dogma' (Seltzer 1976: 14). Not unlike Thorn, Kennedy was not profoundly Catholic (Carty 2004: 4). But if Thorn were successful in his bid, it would make him (post-Kennedy, but pre-Biden) the second only Catholic President in United

States history. Seltzer, prior to writing *The Omen*, had been involved in television political documentaries, including the ABC special *The Unfinished Journey of Robert F. Kennedy* (Mel Stuart, 1970). And with the creation of Robert Thorn he has intimated that he had the Kennedys, specifically Robert Kennedy, in mind (Seltzer n.d.). In making him the United States Ambassador to the United Kingdom, aka the Ambassador of the United States to the Court of St. James, Seltzer is invoking a highly prestigious position that has served as a stepping-stone for later American presidents including John Adams and son, James Monroe, Martin Van Buren and James Buchanan. The position was also held by patriarch (and wannabe president) Joseph P. Kennedy.

1.2 Ambassador Thorn.

Relocating to England for the new position, Kathy gives her husband a tour of the mansion on the outskirts of London. Robert thinks it is a 'bit much', but Kathy is insistent that 'nothing's too much for the wife of the future president of the United States'. Notwithstanding the flippancy of her remark, this announces Robert's political ambitions. Before going upstairs to make love on the hard floor of the unfurnished house, Robert jests, 'You know, you could be too sexy for the White House.' Later, when Robert and Kathy take a walk with Damien through the country estate, we learn of Robert's rich and powerful connections – he quips that he won't have much to talk about with the former college roommate who has since 'assumed the awesome burden of the presidency'. 'Well, give my regards to the First Lady,' rejoins Kathy, passing up the invitation to accompany her husband on a trip to meet with the President to spend time with Damien instead. Such playful, throwaway banter, *obiter dicta*, carries important information and economically establishes the theme of power and the presidential line of succession.

Belonging to a family dynasty, Robert and Katherine Thorn are rich, attractive and photogenic. The trailer helps fill in the gaps: 'For generations, the Thorns have been a family of tremendous wealth, position and power. The perfect marriage of Ambassador Thorn and his wife Katherine was fulfilled by the birth of their son, Damien.' Painted in the broadest strokes, we only find out in *Damien: Omen II* that the family-owned Thorn Industries made their fortune in electronics and energy. As the perfect heterosexual, nuclear family, Robert is the breadwinner father and Kathy the stay-at-home mother, albeit with a nursemaid and servants in her employ. Feminism seems to have hardly touched Robert's younger wife (Remick was twenty years Peck's junior), or at least she has no use for it in her affluent existence. This had led Wood (2003: 79) to note that, on the surface, *The Omen* is 'old-fashioned, traditional, reactionary: the goodness of the family unit isn't questioned; horror is disowned by having the devil-child, a product of the Old World [first Italy then England], unwittingly *adopted* into the American family'. (For Wood, though, the deaths of nearly all the establishment figures by the end masks a radical political agenda.)

This was in a decade where the nuclear family, amid rising divorce rates, Women's Liberation, gay liberation, and youth alienation, was seen to be on the brink of collapse; when one of the first ever reality TV shows, *An American Family* (1973), chronicled the breakdown of a middle-class family. 'By the middle of the decade, fewer than half of married two-parent households, and fewer than one-fourth of all American households, conformed to the nuclear ideal of a breadwinner father and a stay-at-home mother' (Lassiter 2008: 14). Under the attractive frame of 'family values', then, Wood (2004: 79) equates the Thorns with the 'patriarchal, bourgeois capitalist Establishment', which is precisely what is at stake here when we speak of 'the end of world'.

Before *The Final Conflict* wreaked havoc on the timeline of the series, it was reasonable to assume that the events of *The Omen* were contemporaneous i.e., the year 1976 (as para-textually affirmed by the publicity campaign: 'Today is the 6th day of the 6th month of 1976'). On November 2 1976 Republican Gerald Ford narrowly lost the US election to Democrat Jimmy Carter. A member of the Baptist Church and a self-proclaimed born again Christian, Carter positioned himself as a political outsider, as different from Nixon as one could get. 'Promising a new start, Carter refused to embrace the policy orthodoxies to which most Democrats subscribed and promised to challenge the entrenched interests in Washington' (Kruse & Zelizer 2019: 35). However, the one-term president would soon be accused of ineffectual government as he combated the worsening energy crisis, rampant inflation and unemployment. In his now-infamous 'malaise speech' delivered on July 15, 1979, Carter spoke of a 'crisis of confidence' in the land: 'It is a crisis that strikes at the very heart and soul and spirit of our national will. We can see this crisis in the growing doubt about the meaning of our own lives and in the loss of a unity of purpose for our nation.'

As disenchantment for Carter set in, Democrat-turned-Republican Ronald Reagan mobilised the Christian Right, including conservative evangelical Protestants and Roman Catholics, and the more secular New Right in his 1980 presidential campaign. The 'great communicator' railed against welfare spending, the 'soft' approach to crime, moral decay, and big government. To millions of Americans, he offered a message of hope and opportunity that contrasted starkly with Carter's pessimism, while appealing to a belief in 'original sinlessness' or innocence that sought to restore the nation's fabled past (Wills 2000: 448-60). Yet Kruse and Zelizer (2019: 114) write: 'Whatever his powers of persuasion, Reagan alone could not remake the political landscape. The new movements of the 1970s had created a powerful base for conservatism, but liberalism remained a force in national politics. For all its fracturing in the 1970s, the New Deal state dominated.' Moreover, this rightward turn in 1970s American politics wasn't inevitable; it was 'fiercely contested', involving a 'massive mobilization by activists, organisations, and political elites associated with the conservative movement' (Schulman & Zelizer 2008: 3). For Kolker (2011: 279), such films as *Dirty Harry* (Don Siegel, 1971) and *Death Wish* (Michael Winner, 1974) were symptomatic of the growing conservatism of the 1970s, articulating 'the Nixonian calls for law and order against antiwar activists'. These are fault lines that persist to this day.

For a movie about the devil-child's rise in the world of politics, *The Omen* is remarkable for its *lack* of engagement with world events and politics. Reading from a scholarly work, Jennings hashes out with Robert the meaning of the poem, during a pitstop at a roadside cafe in Italy, as they make their way to see Father Spiletto at the monastery. Jennings ventures that: 'The Jews have returned to Zion and there has been a comet. As for the rise of the Roman Empire, scholars think that could well mean the formation of the Common Market, the Treaty of Rome.' Robert, understandably, thinks this sort of speculation is a 'bit of a stretch', and he could well be addressing the implied audience! Jennings is, of course, referring to the establishment of the State of Israel in 1948 and the 1957 treaty that led to the establishment of the European Economic Community, commonly referred to in the 1970s as the Common Market. (For the record, Comet West, otherwise known as the 'great comet', passed through the inner solar system in 1976. This, however, received little media coverage.) And as for the 'eternal sea' mentioned in the poem, Jennings explains that theologians have already interpreted it to mean 'the world of politics, the sea that constantly rages with turmoil and revolution. So, the Devil's child will rise from the world of politics.'

The turmoil would have required no elaboration for 1970s audiences, all-too-familiar with the fallout from Watergate and Vietnam, Arab-Israeli hostilities or the economically crippling oil crisis. Robert, early on, tells his aid that for personal reasons it is not the right time for a trip to Saudi Arabia – perhaps he is worried that Kathy won't cope on her own after the nanny's inexplicable suicide. But otherwise, as Duncan Leigh Cooper (1976-77: 47) commented in *Cineaste*: 'There is no hint in *The Omen* of the real dangers which beset the apparently idyllic world of the Thorns and their class – wars, revolutions, economic collapse. Presumably, a millionaire diplomat, a man with presidential aspirations like Robert Thorn, would be concerned with these problems. Instead, Thorn remains completely obsessed not with real dangers, but with the amorphous menace embodied in a five-year-old child.' As per the scapegoating mechanism described by French cultural critic and philosopher René Girard (2001), the film disavows such dangers and attributes their causes to a devil figure, rendered safely external to the culture and theoretically eradicable. The innocent child is remade into the enemy.

Despite the Kennedy connection, Robert's political affiliation remains vague – the words Democrat or Republican (or, for that matter, Catholic) are never so much as uttered in the film. In the novelisation, Seltzer provides some much-needed background. In a scene that would not have been out of place in the film, Robert addresses businessmen at a hotel, in a speech on the World Economic Structure, the importance of the Common Market, and global inequities in wealth. But as he delivers his speech, he is heckled by a bearded, blue-jeaned young activist, 'likely from the Communist faction' (which we readily associate with the New Left and anti-war college-campus demonstrations of the decade), on the ruling-class hypocrisy of his comments about the evils of luxury born of wealth and position. 'What do you know about poverty, Thorn? … You'll never have to work a day in your life!' Continuing: 'If you're so concerned about sharing your wealth, why don't you share some of yours? … How many millions do you *have*? Do you know how many people are *starving*? …. Don't stand there in your four hundred dollar suit and tell us what poverty is about!' (Seltzer 1976: 82-3). When the heckler presses the ambassador, 'What are you worth, Thorn? … As much as Rockefeller?' (1976: 83), Robert is humbled in front of the audience and forced to admit, 'We should all share our wealth. I'll try to do more' (Seltzer 1976: 84). The scene speaks not only of intergenerational conflict but also of class warfare, implied on some level in the film (see Chapter 3), in which the elder statesman is shown to be out of touch with the plight of third-world countries, but also with the concerns of the younger, radical generation.

1.3 Robert and Jennings engage in some theological speculation about the end times.

Ultimately, of course, Robert Thorn is little more than an instrument, the devil-child's pathway to the presidency. Somewhat perversely, Sabine Büssing (1987: 126) suggests that the fact Robert 'tenderly fosters the child that was imposed on him is in a way paralleled by his bearing as a politician: being an idealistic diplomat who regards his task as a mission for the entire free world, he willingly becomes a slave to foreign forces if he feels he can thus serve his purpose'.

In terms of the play between onscreen/offscreen identity, one may speculate about the extent to which Gregory Peck identified with the Robert Thorn character. A loyal and liberal Democrat, Peck knew and admired JFK, narrating the documentary special *John F. Kennedy: Years of Lightning, Days of Drums* (Bruce Herschensohn, 1966) in memory of the slain president. He was also on the master list of Nixon's political opponents, speaking out against the Vietnam War and active in his support of Democratic campaigns. Critic David Thomson (2016: 803) even goes as far as to say that the Peck persona *is* 'Kennedy-like, preferring to act in crisis, and always cosmetically vindicated'. Espousing a racial liberalism, Peck brought a Kennedyesque integrity to his role of Southern lawyer Atticus Finch defending a black man in *To Kill a Mockingbird*, which thereafter became his signature performance. Indeed, it would not be too much of a stretch to say older sections of the 1970s audience would have brought this bear to on his role as an ambassador. Peck, interestingly, saw himself as ideally suited to the part (Shay 1976: 40). Peck's public faith is further suggestive in light of the character he played. A modern, liberal Roman Catholic, he once contemplated becoming a priest. He essayed one on two occasions: a free-thinking missionary in his second film *The Keys of the Kingdom* (John M. Stahl, 1944; scoring his first Oscar nod), and the real-life Monsignor Hugh O'Flaherty in the made-for-TV *The Scarlet and the Black* (Jerry London, 1983). In late 1978, Peck was one of the guests at the White House when Pope John Paul II came to Washington during Carter's one-term presidency (Haney 2005: 366).

Yet in taking to *The Omen* what one brings to it, some might construe Robert as more of a bedfellow of Nixon or Reagan than Carter, at best a moderate Republican (or pejorative Rockefeller Republican) allied with the business and political elite. And as played by the going-on-sixty Peck, an actor from the Old Hollywood seeking to reinvent himself in the changing landscape of the New Hollywood after the failure of his recent movies, Robert is not exactly a young, vibrant politician for the younger generation; rather, he may stand more for the older order, too old to have been part of the 1960s and 1970s counterculture. As previously discussed, this 'order' would reassert itself in the conservative counter-movements of the 1970s, as galvanised by the religious and secular right. *The Omen* may thus be interpreted as a vehicle for right-wing paranoia, of how the ruling-class establishment is under assault by subversive, left-wing forces.

In retrospect, the political turmoil referred to in the film, symbolised by the 'eternal sea' of Father Brennan's pseudo-religious rhyme, is further suggestive of the ideological war of conservative versus liberal/progressive values in modern American politics. Whether this ends with the destruction of the Establishment from within or a new, reshaped Establishment, a New World Order, depends on how we read Damien and the ending, which I fully unpack in Chapter 3.

CHAPTER 2: THE DEVIL DELUSION

> Here is wisdom. Let him that hath understanding count the number of the beast: for
> it is the number of a man; and his number is six hundred threescore and six.
> – Book of Revelation, chapter 13, verse 18.[3]

In the opening credits of *The Omen*, the silhouetted figure of a little boy appears to
the right-hand side of the frame. Suffused in a hellish glow, the figure casts an unusual
shadow that from one angle is an upright cross or crucifix, and from the other an
inverted cross, the symbol of the Antichrist. These credits are set to Goldsmith's all-
important theme 'Ave Satani' sung in Latin by a choir. Yet before it was co-opted as an
anti-Christian, occult symbol, widely circulated in horror films and heavy metal music, the
inverted or Petrine Cross was associated with the Martyrdom of Peter. As found in the
non-canonical *Acts of Peter*, the famed apostle is reputed to have asked his executioners
to crucify him upside down to be 'symbolic of that man who was first made', and to
reflect his own unworthiness to be crucified in the same manner as Christ (Elliott
1993: 425). The inverted cross has been adopted by some Catholics as a symbol of
martyrdom, of humble Christianity. But in a film that plays fast and loose with religion
and demonology, it is also a fitting signifier for the child's unstable, 'reversible' nature:
fiendish agent versus innocent victim. *The Omen*'s credits thus set the tone of ambiguity,
uncertainty, built into the sophisticated, diplopic nature of the narrative, for the most
part overlooked in readings of the film. Donner himself was adamant that: 'The plot is
built around that [Biblical] prophecy, but we were making a mystery-suspense thriller,
not a Biblical story' (Appelbaum 1976: 31). And despite the shock effects, which Donner
took obvious delight in designing and executing, the narrative was always intended to
have an ambiguous relationship with reality, more psychological than supernatural.

As Donner told Don Shay following the release of the movie: 'I treated the child, in my
mind, right up to the very last frame of the picture, as just a five-year-old kid. He knows
not what he is yet. The Bible says the child will be sired by the rape of a four-legged
beast by Satan. I don't know if that's possible …' He added, 'We treated the whole thing,
as best as we could, as a reality. Everything in it could be coincidental. You never see
anybody create [i.e. commit] an inhuman deed. Liberties are taken, obviously …' (Shay
1976: 46). Similarly, Donner told Ralph Appelbaum that

... my approach was that in a sense we are making two pictures – or rather, one picture open to two different interpretations. If you want to believe that demonic, superhuman forces are controlling the lives of the characters, you can ... [But] If you look at the story more carefully, you'll see that every death, every accident, every bizarre incident, could be the result of natural causes: summer storms, lightning, and so forth. You never see demons or ghoulish figures; it could all be coincidence. And eventually all these horrible coincidences drive the Ambassador crazy. (Appelbaum 1976: 31)

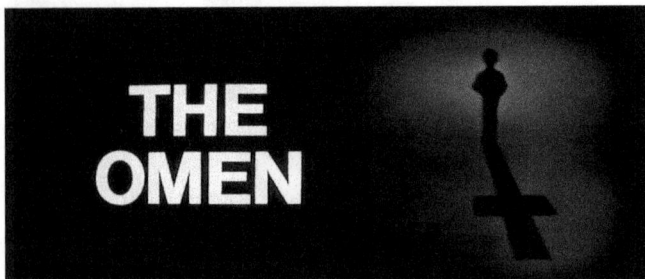

2.1. The striking opening title sequence of The Omen.

Donner may have taken his leaf out Hitchcock's book here, whose films *Rebecca* (1940), *Vertigo* (1958) and *Psycho* (1960) likewise flirt with the supernatural, before settling on a rational/logical explanation. However, a much more direct influence on *The Omen* is again Roman Polanski's masterwork *Rosemary's Baby*. Bothered by the fact there was no real devil in the movie, Polanksi has said that he sought to create a film 'in which the idea of the Devil could be conceived as Rosemary's folly. We never see anything supernatural in it. And everything that occurred that has any kind of supernatural look occurs in her dream, as in the book [by Ira Levin] by the way', adding that 'it could have been all the question of her paranoia, of her suspicions during the pregnancy, and post-partum craze' (*Remembering Rosemary*, 2012). As we shall see, Kathy's estrangement from her changeling son may also be seen as symptomatic of her paranoia.

As per his vision, Donner instructed Seltzer to remove all references in his script to devil-gods, cloven-hoofed beasts, and the like. 'Dick said there must be nothing in this movie that you can't believe isn't actual,' recalls Seltzer. 'The whole force of this movie is going to be the critical mass, of a man's paranoia coming to be realised as actual. And every single event, every single death, could be seen as the kind of freak accident that could occur in the real world' (*The Omen Legacy*, 2001). As we saw, the accidental or coincidental aspect was driven home in Fox's theatrical trailer, overseen by Donner. For his part, Seltzer has said: 'What I wanted to do with *The Omen* is deal in the delusion of the Devil, and the fantasy and the imagination. Because these things that really frighten us are those things that make us think we are losing our mind' (*666: The Omen Revealed*, 2000). By his own admission, the finished film was a major improvement on his original script. And whereas the film has the hallmarks of a paranoid conspiracy thriller, the novelisation is much more on the nose; 'horror fiction, through and through' (Guariento 2019: 70). In producer Harvey Bernhard's mind there was never any doubt that Damien was the Antichrist.

Much as the name 'Damien' suggests the tortured Father Damien from *The Exorcist*, still present in people's minds at the time of *The Omen*'s release, Seltzer had in mind Belgian Catholic missionary Father Damien, who was stationed in Hawaii in the late nineteenth century. He became lionised for his work with lepers on the island of Molokai, ultimately succumbing to the disease in 1889 (his story has been filmed more once, including in 1999 as *Molokai: The Story of Father Damien*, directed by Paul Cox). He was canonised by Pope Benedict XVI in 2009. The saintly aspect of his namesake thus lends an additional note of irony to little Damien's characterisation, as does the surname 'Thorn', which evokes Christ's woven Crown of Thorns vis-à-vis his crucifixion.

To help illumine our understanding of the ambiguous nature of *The Omen*'s narrative, I turn to Tzvetan Todorov's formalist/structuralist approach to 'the fantastic' as a literary genre. For Todorov, the experience of the fantastic is defined by the ambiguity or hesitation between the real and imaginary, truth and illusion. This is determined by our understanding of the laws of nature. Thus:

> In a world which is indeed our world, the one we know, a world without devils, sylphides, or vampires, there occurs an event which cannot be explained by the laws of this same familiar world. The person who experiences the event must opt for one of two possible solutions: either he is a victim of an illusion of the senses, of a product of the imagination – and laws of the world then remain what they are; or else the

> event has indeed taken place, it is an integral part of reality – but then this reality is
> controlled by laws unknown to us. Either the devil is an illusion, an imaginary being; or
> else he really exists, precisely like other living things – with this reservation, that we
> encounter him infrequently. (Todorov 1975: 25)

But if the person can choose between these solutions, then s/he must leave Todorov's
realm of the fantastic and turn to one of its neighbouring genres: the uncanny
(supernatural explained; via dreams, madness, drugs, intoxication, deception or fraud) or
the marvellous (supernatural accepted).

Some narratives, Todorov suggests, sustain 'their ambiguity to the very end, i.e. even
beyond the narrative itself' (1975: 43), as in Henry James' psychological-cum-ghost
story *The Turn of the Screw* (1898; filmed in 1961 by Jack Clayton as *The Innocents*). Here,
James asks us to consider two possible solutions for the events in the story: one that
the children under the governess's care are possessed by the spirits of the maid and
manservant (the marvellous), and the other that the spirits are the products of her
diseased imagination (the uncanny). The ambiguity between these opposing explanations
renders the child as both innocent and evil, victim and villain (Schober 2004: 55). And
furthermore, it turns the child into the site of tensions between Romantic conceptions
of childhood innocence, as espoused by Romantic poets like William Blake and William
Wordsworth, and the notion of original sin of Evangelical/Puritan ideology (Schober
2004: 1-7). Seltzer believes that the secret of *The Omen* was that 'it centred around an
innocent villain. This kid who did not know he was the Devil's child, who did not know
he was causing the chaos around him. Somebody who was vulnerable as he was evil'
(*Screenwriter's Notebook* 2004). The innocent villain corresponds to Sabine Bussing's
(1987: 101) notion of the 'evil innocent' who 'is never fully conscious of the harmful things
that happen through it – and sometimes to it– and notably has no awareness of any
metamorphoses within its own soul'. Or Damien may, in fact, be an innocent human child,
an 'innocent innocent'. In any case, the ambiguity behind this device, Jamesian in intention
and effect, was abandoned (Seltzer thinks squandered) by the producers of the sequels.

Based on these statements about intention in which ambiguity was wittingly built into
The Omen text, we may postulate four lines of interpretation or scenarios, each carrying
different suppositions:

1.	There is a Satanic conspiracy, Damien is the Devil's offspring, and the Devil is a real entity. Therefore, Damien is evil. (*The marvellous.*)

2.	There is a Satanic conspiracy, Damien is *not* the Devil's offspring, and the Devil is *not* a real entity. Therefore, Damien is innocent. (*The uncanny.*)

3.	There isn't a Satanic conspiracy, Damien is not the Devil's offspring, and the Devil is not a real entity. Therefore, he is innocent. (*The uncanny.*)

4.	There is a Satanic conspiracy, Damien is the Devil's offspring, and the Devil is a real entity. And Damien is an 'innocent villain'. (*The marvellous.*)

The first interpretation seems to make the most intuitive sense. The second and third would be reading against the grain, while the final – and perhaps most subtle – interpretation has been suggested by Seltzer himself. Somewhat counter-intuitively, yet fully consistent with Donner's double vision, I wish to entertain the second scenario, based on paranoia or hysteria – i.e. a Devil delusion.

However, while each of these interpretations revolves around Damien, there is good reason to consider *The Omen* Robert's – and not Damien's – story. The character appears in about 80 per cent of scenes, and he is closest to being the focalizer, the main character through which the story unfolds, beginning in a hospital in Rome in which he helps set off a chain of events that climaxes on the altar of a church in England. In one respect, Damien is little more than a MacGuffin, in the Hitchcockian sense (Scahill 2012: 99): the driver for the plot, triggering the characters to either protect (as in Mrs Baylock's case) or destroy him (as in the case of Robert, Jennings or Bugenhagen), or circumvent his malign influence. And as Kathy Merlock Jackson (1986: 145) remarks, 'Damien has very little on-screen presence: what is said about him takes on greater importance than what he actually says and does.' Which is to say he is an *absent presence*. Apropos of the second scenario, I wish to test Donner's idea that a series of unfortunate events or coincidences coupled with the 'misguided' motives of a Satanic coven drives Peck's ambassador into madness and folly. Such a reading is valuable because it shows up *The Omen*'s ambiguous textual and stylistic effects and features, depending on the Todorovian (and Jamesian) hesitation between the twin genres of the uncanny and marvellous that is the very essence of the fantastic.

In both *Rosemary's Baby* and *The Omen*, wives are duped by their husbands into harbouring the son of Satan. But whereas Rosemary's actor husband Guy Woodhouse enters into a Faustian pact, in effect selling his wife's body to a Satanic coven in return for their intervention in his career, Robert is motivated by a deep, selfless love for his wife that leads him to spare her the truth about their still-born baby – or so they have been told. He thus consents to an under-the-table adoption without her knowledge; an act of love born of duplicity. While adding a fascinating complication to their relationship, it was this aspect of the plot that Peck found so troubling. While acknowledging that the script 'held my interest like a good pulp thriller', despite its many plot holes, he thought 'Thorn was far too intelligent to accept a substitute child, and without looking into the background of the adoptee, and certainly he would have told his wife about it. Also, Satan could easily have substituted his child for ours without telling Thorn about the switch. The Thorns would have been the innocent victims of the conspiracy' (Shay 1976: 40). Additionally, Robert would have almost certainly asked to have seen his son's body before making the switcheroo; as it is, he takes everything at face value from Father Spiletto.

Indeed, so strongly did Peck feel about this point that he lobbied Donner, Seltzer and Bernhard to have it changed based on his unassailable logic – to appease the actor they cut the scene the other way – but was overruled (Fishgall 2002: 289-290). In their view, it worked better with Robert having to live with the guilt for his well-meaning lie; one is inclined to agree. One suspects that the Hollywood icon – known for his somewhat dour portrayals of men of integrity, including priests and lawyers – was worried about the fallout for his carefully cultivated screen persona. In turning the story into a meditation on personal guilt, more palpable than any 'free-floating' Catholic guilt, Donner and Seltzer were able to point to fascinating cracks in the integrity of this persona. It is this aspect of *The Omen* that elevates it from the merely horrific to the tortured and Gothic.

PICTURE-PERFECT FAMILY

The adoption scene at the Catholic hospital, unfolding under a cloak of secrecy and silence, sets up important motivation for character and plot. Robert confides to Father

Spiletto, 'I'm afraid it will kill her. My God, she wanted a baby so much. For such a long time … What can I tell her? What …can I say?' It's obvious that he fears she will suffer some sort of breakdown. When Father Spiletto suggests they adopt, Robert indicates that Kathy wanted her own. A while later, we see Robert reflected in the glass partition of the maternity ward as one of the sisters carries the wrapped baby in her arms. Before Donner pulls focus the image of Robert is blurred, suggesting a blurred vision of reality; it's as if he is looking through a glass darkly, not quite recognising what he sees – and is about to do. The glass thus becomes a symbol of self-reflection, *self-judgement*. As the camera pulls back, the dark-robed Spiletto slips into the reflection like an evil serpent, saying, 'If I may suggest, it even resembles … Your wife need never know. It would be a blessing to her … and to the child.' Robert receives assurances that the child has no relatives, but Robert's face, as conveyed by Peck with splendid nuance, shows how conflicted he really is.

2.2. In the maternity ward, Robert looks through a glass a darkly at his child to be.

The following scene has Robert cradling the baby, for all appearances normal and healthy, which he brings over to the radiant Kathy in her hospital bed. As she holds the newborn, they kiss lovingly, underscored by Goldsmith's tender 'love theme' (set to lyrics on the soundtrack album as 'The Piper Dreams', sung by Goldsmith's wife). Some time elapses and Damien is now a toddler being dressed on the table by his mother. Kathy reacts to her husband's joyous news, relayed with faux nonchalance, that he has just been appointed ambassador to Great Britain.

'I wanted to do [the film] from the standpoint of complete normality,' Donner said at the time. 'That's why the first eight minutes are so important because they show the happy, adjusted marriage of Gregory Peck and Lee Remick, the perfectly ordinary world into which this terror comes' (Castell 1976: 103). But not so happy, well-adjusted, it would seem, given Robert's unease about his wife's fragility, if not instability in the exchange between him and Father Spiletto; only later, when she asks him to find her a psychiatrist, can we surmise that Kathy has a history of anxiety and/or depression. The novelisation is more forthcoming on this point: two miscarriages and acute stress brought on by her inability to 'cope with the duties of a politician's wife' have taken their toll, resulting in acts of self-harm that led Kathy to seek a psychiatrist (Seltzer 1976: 8).

In his noted study, *Hearths of Darkness: The Family in the American Horror Film*, Tony Williams (2014: 118) asserts: 'Without Satanic explanation *The Omen* could have profitably developed the theme of parental insecurity over child rearing. However, it moves toward old Puritanistic scapegoating tendencies.' That is to say, evil in the child is safely attributed to demonic agency. Making comparisons with *The Exorcist*, Williams (2014: 115) writes that the film 'lacks its flawed counterpart's productive ambiguities' with Damien rendered as Satan's offspring. This seems difficult to defend, given the ambiguities built into the narrative by Donner and Seltzer; Damien may, after all, be an innocent human child. Later, he equivocates further, suggesting the equivocal nature of the text itself: '*The Omen* attacks all of Western civilization's cherished institutions – family, religion, and politics – transforming them into microcosmic facets of death and armageddon. The manifest explanation emphasizes demonic agency, but other textual factors suggest paranoid feelings toward children' (Williams 2014: 118). In linking these feelings to 1970s discourses of children/childhood, I have argued elsewhere that possessed and satanic child narratives speak most to middle- to upper-class anxieties about childhood unbound, and swing between the poles of protectiveness and paedophobia (Schober 2004: 166). In any case, the way *The Omen* mines parental paranoia doesn't necessarily negate the Satanic interpretation.

For one, the film suggests how we might not be keeping a close enough watch on our children, whose lives may be in danger, which is also the underlying message of Fritz Lang's thriller *M* (1931) or Robert Wise's reincarnation melodrama *Audrey Rose* (1977). Early on, Donner renders the Thorns' familial bliss in a somewhat mawkish montage over Goldsmith's lush treatment of the love theme, previewed earlier. At their new residence in England, Robert and Kathy go for an idyllic walk on the country estate, with little Damien in tow. But what happens next underlines the fragility of this bliss; how it can all change in an instant. So deeply involved in each other, they forget about Damien's whereabouts (who has been out of the frame for some time). 'Where is he?' asks Robert. Kathy: 'He was right behind us …' Goldsmith's fraught strings alert us to something frightful, as they desperately call out for Damien and search for him in the rushing creek. His toy dog on wheels sits ominously on the bank. Playing into every parents' worst fears, we half-expect his lifeless body to turn up on in the water. Kathy becomes increasingly alarmed, at which point Damien is spotted next to a tree, smiling innocently. Robert and Kathy share a joyful sigh. And Kathy rushes over to the little boy, 'You little monkey, don't you *ever* do that again.' Damien starts to cry. But whose fault is this?

2.3 Frantic with worry, Robert and Kathy search for Damien.

Labouring the point about the Thorns being a picture-perfect family, Donner presents us with a slideshow of stills ('happy snaps') of their various outings together. The strains of a music box playing 'Happy Birthday to You' segue into the occasion of Damien's fifth birthday party, when the troubles begin. Holly, the nanny, holds Damien in her arms as he blows out the candles on his cake, and the birthday song is sung to him by scores of children and worthies inside the Thorns' circle. As we would expect for the birthday of a rich ambassador's son, this is an elaborate affair, with a carousel, tents and amusements on the lawns of the estate. No doubt seeing a valuable photo op, the Thorns have invited press photographers, including Keith Jennings.

But at the party we sense that Holly poses some sort of threat to the stability of the family, at least in Kathy's mind. Watching as a photographer takes photos of Holly holding

Damien in her arms, she is troubled, for some unfathomable reason; is it because of the undue attention being accorded to her nanny by the press? Or does she feel jealous of the closeness of her relationship with her 'son'? Or perhaps threatened by the younger, attractive woman? In any case, Kathy takes Damien from Holly; and, as underplayed by Holly Palance, her face hints at rejection, hurt. (In an unused scene from a draft of the screenplay, Kathy later confesses to Robert that she feels responsible for what transpires; 'She was getting a lot of attention … and I was jealous of it. I took Damien from her because I couldn't stand sharing center stage' [Seltzer 1975: 15-A]).

2.4 The slighted nanny, Holly (Holly Palance), at the birthday party.

Right after Jennings takes her picture, Holly is transfixed – one might say 'possessed' – by a Rottweiler on the grounds. The significance of dogs as hell-hounds has, of course, a rich history: the three-headed dog Cerberus that guards the Gates of Hell in Greek myth, the dog as witch's familiar, or the black dog of British folklore (as in Arthur Conan Doyle's Sherlock Holmes story, The Hound of the Baskervilles, published in 1902) whose appearance was seen to be a portent of death, as it appears to be here. Donner alternates with close-ups of eyes of both nanny and dog (a device he will repeat almost ad nauseam in the film), which is underscored by ominous music. In the shape of a dog, the eyes convey demonic intelligence or intent, recalling the hoary legend or curse of the Evil Eye that was said to cause misfortune to the receiver. But could these 'effects' belie what is actually happening on screen? Or to recast a well-known quote, is a dog is a dog is a dog? Holly is acting hypnotically or irrationally when she beckons Damien from the roof of the mansion with a noose around her neck: 'Damien, look at me! I'm over here … Damien, I love you! … Look at me, Damien. It's all for you!' Then she jumps, breaking her neck; her body swings back as she smashes through the window. Children

2.5 *The eyes have it in* The Omen.

scream. And as her body dangles lifelessly, Donner lingers on their reactions to this Le Théâtre du Grand-Guignol. This is eclipsed by silence; calliope music from the carousel plays incongruously. Jennings, meanwhile, snaps away.

Through this act, the first of the film's much-talked-about set pieces, the nanny seems to be making a sacrifice in the name of the devil-child – or could she be unhinged to begin with, her slighting by Kathy pushing her over the edge? As Kathy, Damien and Robert huddle together, Damien is transfixed by the Rottweiler in the distance. Once again, Donner alternates between close-ups of eyes. But, as coupled with Goldsmith's cue, is this *necessarily* a diabolic communion? Is the little boy's wave to the animal the wave of an evil innocent, or – deferring to the principle of Occam's razor – innocent? The point is that Donner allows enough latitude here to read the scene ambiguously.

The next day, as he makes his way to the American embassy in London, Robert is assailed by reporters seeking further information on the nanny's 'suicide'. Robert denies the allegation that she left a suicide note or that she used drugs ('Not that I know of'). To be sure, Holly's death is freakish, mystifying, but not – as Donner and Seltzer were careful to establish – a violation of the known laws of reality. Ergo, we may defer to a more rational – or uncanny – explanation.

MORE STRANGE INCIDENTS

On the same day Robert receives a visit from a Father Brennan from Rome at the embassy, over a matter of 'urgent, personal business'. Wasting no time on pleasantries, the Father tells Robert to accept Christ as his saviour and to take Communion, for 'only if he is within you, can you defeat the son of the Devil … He's killed once, he'll kill again. He'll kill until everything that's yours is his …' At this point, Thorn calls over the intercom for a security guard to remove him from the office. But in increasingly hysterical tones, the priest refuses to be interrupted as he tells the ambassador that he was present at the hospital the night his son was born – 'I witnessed the birth' – and saw his/its mother. Robert insists that it was his wife he saw and demands to know what he wants ('If this is blackmail, then come out and say it …'). At this precise moment, the Father tells him that 'His mother was a ja – ', but he is cut off in the cacophony of voices as a guard proceeds to eject him. An earlier draft of the screenplay has him clearly say 'jackal' (as it is rendered in the novelisation), but Donner shrewdly holds off on this piece of information for later. Outside Jennings takes a photograph of the downtrodden, diminutive priest as he leaves the embassy.

As hammed up by Troughton, we could dismiss the cleric's brogue ravings as those of a religious fanatic, or even madman. But, from Robert's point of view, can we so easily dismiss the possibility that he knows something about the unusual circumstances of Damien's true parentage and subsequent adoption? Robert suspects blackmail; a payment for the priest's silence over revelations that could cause irreparable harm to both his marriage and political career. But if Brennan is not a madman, not a blackmailer, then could his ravings have some basis in empirical fact? Out of this hesitation or uncertainty between the uncanny and the marvellous, the upstanding ambassador will find his own rational, coherent worldview increasingly tested – and upended.

After the tragedy of Damien's nanny, the arrival of her austere, middle-aged replacement Mrs Baylock seems like a 'godsend'. Her accent – like that of Father Brennan – marks her out as Irish (and *prima facie* Catholic). She confidently inserts herself into the household as a panacea to Kathy and Robert's recent troubles, without attachments, or 'boyfriend troubles – I left that a long time ago'. She urges Kathy and Robert to let her and Damien 'get acquainted in our own way', despite his shyness with meeting new people. Mrs Baylock engenders confidence, so much so they almost forget to inquire about the circumstances of her arrival. She claims, imprecisely, that she was sent by 'the agency' after they read about the news of the previous nanny. We never do learn whether Kathy confirmed her story with the agency or had her references checked.

2.6 Mrs Baylock inserts herself into the Thorn household.

The following scene appears to establish a diabolic communion between the new nanny and her new charge. As Damien lies on the nursery floor in front of the fireplace, bathed in the flickering glow of the fire à la the opening, he looks up from his drawing to the strange visitor. In a low-angle shot, we see only Mrs Baylock's legs and shoes, as she intones conspiratorially, 'Have no fear, little one, I am here to protect thee.' Damien also smiles up at her conspiratorially, at least as it's italicised by Goldsmith's rendering of 'Ave Satani' on piano. Framed in a long shot through the darkened hallway, she closes the nursery door. In short, Mrs Baylock exudes menace from the outset, which seems to code her as evil, part of a Satanic plot that once included Father Spiletto and Father Brennan. But is Damien's smile here *necessarily* conspiratorial? Richard Combs (1976: 170) was led to observe that the devil-child – if we can even call him that – 'remains a mere sweetly smiling cypher'.

Donner, in fact, expresses sympathy for the little devil, and repeatedly calls on us to see him more as a victim than victimiser. This is exemplified in the sequence where Damien accompanies Kathy and Robert to a church wedding. Back at the house, Kathy has a confrontation of sorts with Mrs Baylock, who obliquely resists her instructions to have Damien dressed and ready: 'Well, excuse me for speaking my mind, ma'am, but do you really think a five-year-old will understand the goings-on of an Episcopal wedding?' Kathy will live to rue her decision. As they ride in a chauffeured car to the neo-Gothic cathedral, Kathy and Robert become increasingly concerned about Damien's emotional state. Robert asks, 'Something wrong?' Kathy replies, 'He seems – I don't know – he just seems scared to death.' Robert wonders if he is ill. While on the surface the sequence doesn't appear to carry any obvious menace or threat, Stuart Baird's carefully paced

2.7 En route to the church.

editing, coupled with Goldsmith's off-kilter chimes, woodwinds and strings contribute to the mounting apprehension. As the car comes to a stop outside the cathedral, Donner zooms in on the golden angel on top of the tower through the car's side window, a *magnification* of Damien's optical point of view, attended by a surge of 'Ave Satani' – and silence. Then Damien bursts into hysterics, pummelling Kathy and pulling her hair, crying 'No!' Only Robert can restrain him, as he tells his chauffer to drive on, while the wedding guests look on in horror and bewilderment. To be sure, the attack – tantrum – is notable for its ferocity; we wouldn't *normally* expect such behaviour from a five-year-old. But it's also not out of the realm of possibility either, if we look to actual examples of children with behavioural and anti-social disorders. What's more, Damien here reacts more like a wild animal threatened.

IDÉE FIXE

With the coincidences piling up quickly, Thorn begins to suspect that something is not quite right with the child. When he asks Kathy, as she nurses her wounds after the attack in the car, if they should have a doctor examine Damien, she assures him that he is 'just fine'. She of course has no way of knowing Damien is not the true issue of their union; that he is, in fact, an imposter child, and therefore an unknown quantity. She is also unaware of Robert's encounter with Father Brennan, which has left him rattled – and rightly so. Kathy insists that Damien is 'perfectly alright – never been sick a day in his life', which only further fuels his suspicions: 'He never has, has he? … Isn't that a little strange? … I mean, no measles, or mumps, or chickenpox. Not even a cough or cold.' But Kathy's so-called maternal instinct wins out here, even though the child is not her flesh and blood: 'Look, he's a perfectly healthy boy. I mean, we have nothing to worry about with him. Not physically … or otherwise. He just had a bad moment. You know, like a fright.'

But the idea has already taken hold in Robert's mind, and is symptomatic of his gradual descent into paranoia. Paranoia was once used interchangeably with monomania to denote an irrational obsession or fixation with an idea. French clinicians of the nineteenth century termed this the *idée fixe*. As theorised by French psychologist Pierre Janet (1859-1947), these ideas develop involuntarily or subconsciously, and are often the result of trauma or a heightened state of suggestibility:

> The trauma-induced emotion is a pathological phenomenon that leads to exhaustion of the individual, that is, a weakening of her or his psychological energies, or mental tension and force. This weakening of mental tension and force causes a diminution of psychological synthesis, thereby facilitating the formation of fixed ideas. This process is called *désaggregation* or dissociation.

> In the simplest case, fixed ideas are the clinical symptom, that is, the re-experiencing of a life event by the individual, and these ideas bear a close relation to an unequivocally stressful event. However, very frequently the causality is more complicated because the clinical symptom – or the fixed idea – has no recognizable relation to any stressful event. In a case like this, the traumatic event did not cause the fixed idea, but weakened psychological tension and force so that a [sic] earlier fixed idea reappears. (Heim & Bühler 2006: 115)

For Robert, a series of traumatic events and bizarre encounters leads to a weakening of his 'psychological constitution', hence heightened suggestibility, resulting in the formation of the *idée fixe*. At the same time, this idea relates to trauma-related guilt over his role in Damien's closet adoption.

Father Brennan, in the throes of his own monomania, of course has his own *idée fixe* that foments Robert's own. He waylays his quarry at a rugby match, organising a 2:30pm appointment at Bishops Park on the following day, while pressing on him the urgency of his mission. Earlier Robert has noticed him in the vicinity of his stately home. Keeping to the appointment, he finds him seated on a bench on the embankment walkway. Almost

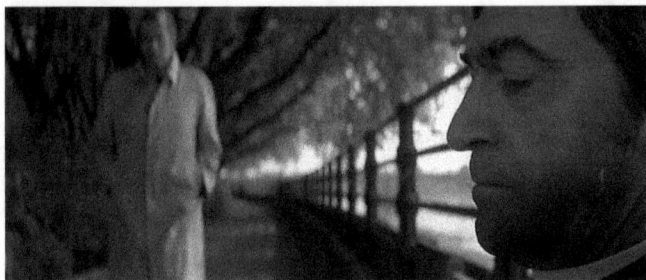

2.8 Father Brennan (Patrick Troughton) tries to warn Robert about Damien's destiny.

at once the priest lets loose his religious doggerel ('When the Jews return to Zion
…'), before telling him that 'the Book of Revelations [sic] predicted it all'. While
Robert declares he's not here to listen to a sermon, the Father ignores his repeated
interjections to give him an alarming forewarning of diabolic succession, one that begins
in the House of Thorn and ends in nothing short of world domination.

He tells Robert that Kathy is pregnant, and that Damien will stop at nothing to kill his
unborn child, then Kathy, and then himself. 'With your wealth and power, he will establish
his counterfeit kingdom here on Earth, receiving his power directly from Satan!' He also
tells Robert to go and see Bugenhagen in Megiddo to receive instructions on how to kill
the son of the Devil, i.e. Damien.

We know that such a forewarning has long stoked the fears of Christian groups and
idiosyncratic sects, if we fail to recognise the so-called signs of the Beast. But for Robert,
this is much more personal, involving a prediction about his unborn child. For his own
perceived failure to convince Robert of Damien's destiny, the Father envisions eternal
damnation for them both.

Following his encounter with the ambassador, the Father is caught in a freakish
windstorm, reminiscent of the storm seemingly conjured up by a black magician in
Jacques Tourneur's supernatural thriller Night of the Demon aka Curse of the Demon
(1957). This veritable tempest is underscored by Goldsmith with Gregorian chants
and primeval driving rhythms that sound suspiciously like the 'Augurs of Spring' section
to Stravinsky's Rite of Spring (1913). As he runs for his life, the priest narrowly avoids
being struck by lightning. He tries to seek refuge in a nearby church. Then, as a lightning

rod from the church is dislodged by lightning, Donner utilises quick analytic cut-ins of the priest's wide-open face and mouth, before homing in on his eyes as he is impaled upright. At this precise moment, a weird serenity prevails. Although this weather-induced event ostensibly denotes demonic agency, it nonetheless remains within the realm of possibility. 'Such things do happen,' according to Seltzer in *The Omen Legacy* (2001). 'As a matter of fact, the impaling came from a story in New York where I was living at the time; somebody had been impaled by a cross that fell from the top of a church.' (Alas, my researches were unable to confirm the truth of this incident.)

'I HAVE SUCH FEARS'

Katherine Thorn has her own story of paranoia that unfolds alongside, and overlaps with, Robert's. Despite her earlier defence of Damien after his wild 'tantrum' in the car on the way to the church, Kathy nurses second thoughts after her terrifying ordeal with Damien at a safari park (filmed on location at the now-closed Windsor Safari Park, billed as 'The Great Adventure', in Windsor, Berkshire). Kathy is at first unsettled by the sight of some giraffes retreating in terror from the boy, or so it seems. Then, as she drives with Damien through the open-air enclosure of the park, she reacts in terror as the car is ferociously set upon by baboons from all directions. Quick cuts from different angles, some hand-held camera and Goldsmith's Stravinskyan score all contribute to a sequence that is riveting and viscerally effective. But Kathy, significantly, is not the only one who is terrified here. So, too, is little Damien. As per his modus operandi, Donner treats the child more as victim than victimiser, preserving the fundamental ambiguity of the narrative.

Kathy's growing suspicions and fears about Damien bespeaks cracks in the white, patriarchal, bourgeois capitalist façade of the American family. When Robert presses her about something being 'wrong', she sounds resigned to the point of despair: 'What's wrong? What could be wrong with our child, Robert?' We're beautiful people, aren't we?' In some vague way, he also suspects Damien. But, while he is the ever-the-attentive husband and she the loving wife it's clear they keep secrets from one another. Robert asks, 'Kathy. Is it so serious?', enfolding her in his large, masculine embrace. Indeed, it is. Worried about her our own mental decline (and there is good reason to suspect that she's gone down this path before), it is Kathy herself who ask him to find her a

2.9 Kathy reveals her fears to Robert.

psychiatrist. 'I have fears. I have such fears', she expresses. And when Robert probes into the nature of those fears, she refuses to elaborate: 'Oh, if I told, you'd put me away.'

But when we encounter Kathy again at the house, she has sunk further into depression and despair. As she sits on the couch, she is increasingly upset by Damien's boisterous play. Robert enters the room, and proceeds to horse around with the animated tyke; perfectly normal father-son behaviour. But we sense Kathy's rising frustration as she orders Mrs Baylock to take him away, notwithstanding Robert's gentle protestation that he's 'only playing'. As he leaves, Damien has a contrite look on his face, as if to say, 'I'm sorry, mummy.' Portrayed realistically to the end, this doesn't fit with our conception of a child bent on humankind's destruction. Could he be just a child?

Through the visual motif of reflections people cast in windows or glass Donner reveals the hidden truth and mental states of his characters. Kathy confides her deepest fears to Robert in front of the window as it rains outside, and she is the one mainly reflected. This echoes the early shot of Robert reflected in the glass partition of the hospital as the nun holds his about-to-be-adopted baby in her arms. Implying that her doctor may be doing more harm than good, Robert thinks it's high time he speaks to him. When Kathy tells him that she doesn't want any more children, she seeks his approval for an abortion, making the startling admission, 'I'm pregnant, Robert. I just found out this morning.' Robert then receives an anonymous phone call (presumably from Jennings) telling him to check the newspapers before hanging up; on the front page is the headline: 'Priest Impaled in Bizarre Tragedy.' The ambassador's mind must be reeling!

2.10 Kathy tells Robert that she's pregnant.

In contrast to Robert's masculine-coded monomania, Kathy seems particularly prone to that 'female malady' described by neurologist Jean-Martin Charcot and his most famous student Freud: hysteria. As derived from the Greek for *hystera* or uterus, referring to the 'disturbance of the womb', hysteria was thought to be a disease of the nervous system triggered by emotional or physical trauma, occurring in far more women than men, and consisting of such symptoms as ovarian sensitivity, pain and fits (Showalter 1997: 33). In the opening, we recall, Robert tells Father Spiletto that his wife wanted a child of her own, and that it would kill her to learn that the baby has died on delivery. That being so, Kathy's psychiatrist notably puts the burden of having a child on Robert: 'Well, she knew how much you wanted one. Now she can't cope. She searches for reasons that won't make her feel inadequate. She has these fantasies. She fantasises that your child is alien, that your child is evil.' Because of her precarious emotional state, he thinks it would be 'disastrous' if she followed through with the pregnancy. When Robert seeks further clarification – 'In what away, evil?' – clearly giving the idea careful consideration, the doctor adds, 'Now, this is just a fantasy. She also thinks the child isn't hers.' Such a fantasy, which in Freud's time would be explained as a form of hysteria, would probably today be diagnosed as a type of post-partum psychosis, characterised by delusions (namely a 'changeling delusion') and disturbances of mood, which can recur during a further pregnancy. When Robert mentions that it was foretold to him that the pregnancy would be terminated and that he is going to fight to see that it's not, the good doctor could be forgiven for thinking that he also needs to be treated for his own fantasies. Robert cuts the interview short, sensing impending danger as he drives home recklessly.

Despite flirting with explanations of paranoia and fantasy, Kathy may be the sanest person in the movie. While Damien's 'evilness' may have no basis in reality, we may infer that she senses he is not her biological son, is an imposter in the household, hence her feelings of estrangement. As Penelope Gilliatt (1978: 86) noted of diabolic child films of the 1970s, with 'their emphasis on misplaced children, these films play on every parent's fear that identification bracelets may have been muddled in the maternity hospital'. Unbeknownst to Kathy, Damien is literally not hers; he *is* a changeling. Damaged by her husband's well-meaning lie, her paranoia is therefore not groundless; as Freud is reputed to have said somewhere, 'the paranoid is never entirely mistaken'.

Following Robert's meeting with the psychiatrist, Kathy suffers a fall from the second floor of the mansion, in another one of the film's most talked-about – and strikingly staged – sequences. As Damien rides his tricycle in circles in the nursery, Kathy tends to a hanging plant from the second-floor landing. She places a fish bowl on top of the balustrade and uses the table to stand on in order to reach the plant. It's precarious, to say the least. Mrs Baylock, looking suitably conspiratorial, allows the child to gather momentum before 'releasing' him onto the landing, and on to his mother. Effective cross-cutting between Damien, Mrs Baylock (including her 'malevolent' eyes) and Kathy draws the suspense out unbearably. In a pre-echo of little Danny Torrance on his tricycle in *The Shining* (Stanley Kubrick, 1980), Donner employs low-angle dolly shots of Damien as he rides helter-skelter, before colliding with Kathy on the table, who goes over the balustrade. The bowl crashes to the floor in slow motion in cascades of water. Kathy clings onto the balusters for dear life, crying 'Damien, Damien!' and 'No, NO!' which seems to be both a cry for help and a condemnation. (The way Donner shoots her through the balusters here vaguely recalls the earlier shot of Robert and Father Spiletto in the anteroom of the Catholic hospital, mentioned earlier.) Kathy loses her grip and falls 'balletically' to the floor, alongside the fish bowl. It is a startling trick shot.[4] This is followed by another close-up of the nanny's eyes, pulling out of focus. Dissolve to a close-up of Kathy's face, blood seeping from her mouth.

Despite the diabolic overtones of the sequence (Goldsmith's score, as always, seems to leave little room for doubt), what is most interesting here is Damien's response afterwards. Ebert (1976: 63) mentions the 'look of sublime happiness on the little boy's face' after almost killing his mother with the tricycle. Yet the boy's expression is much

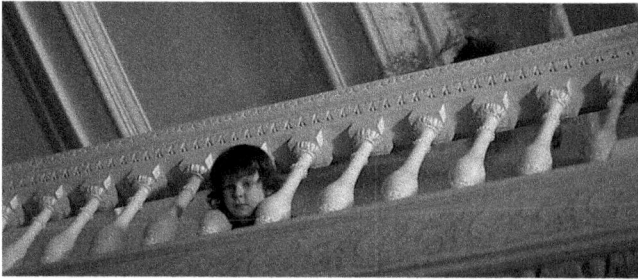

2.11 *Damien as an exercise in ambiguity.*

more enigmatic. Indeed, I would say his face is almost a 'blank', creating in the interaction of shots a kind of Kuleshov effect.[5] As the plant swings eerily overhead, he kneels down and sticks his head through the balusters to see what he's done – is it a look of incomprehension, astonishment, fear or 'happiness'? He slowly stands up. Cut to a God's-eye view of Kathy's lifeless body splayed out on the floor, presumably from Damien's point of view. And then a shot of him running away – like a frightened little boy. It's hardly behaviour we'd expect from the Antichrist. In Seltzer's oxymoronic conception Damien is an innocent villain, unaware of the evil he causes. But could he actually be innocent? Could Kathy's fall be the result of an 'accident,' albeit spurred on by the evil machinations of Mrs Baylock?

When Robert arrives at the hospital, he finds Kathy in intensive care after suffering a concussion, fracture, and internal bleeding. While Robert is justifiably devastated, the treating doctor is somewhat taken aback by his over-concern for the loss of the unborn child. As Robert goes to her bedside, Kathy pleas, 'Don't let him kill me. Don't let him kill me.' By now, Kathy's fears have merged into his own. During a subsequent visit, Kathy tells him she's frightened. He tries to soothe her, only for her to ask, 'What about Damien?' 'I'll speak to Mrs Horton,' he says, 'she'll look after him.' He must think Mrs Baylock is somehow involved, for why would he arrange for the housekeeper to look after him and not the nanny? Kathy's question is also curious at this point; for as far as we know, Damien has just tried to kill her. It even has a ring of motherly concern. Robert later learns from Mrs Baylock that the Hortons have left his employ without notice.

STRANGE COINCIDENCE?

Jennings has arrived at his conspiracy theory independently, and part of the pleasure is in watching how his story and Robert's will eventually intersect. As the hard-nosed freelance photographer (or paparazzo, if we are less kind) who comes to believe in the unbelievable, he plays the role of detective. As Newton (2020: 78) points out, 'the great figure of "knowing" is the detective, and the paranoid fiction is a close cousin of the detective story, though it lacks the latter's rational and comforting quality'. At Damien's fifth birthday party, Jennings mordantly remarks to another invited photographer that he is saving his film for the boy's canonisation, adding, 'I don't know if we just got the heir to the Thorn millions here or Jesus Christ himself' (a nice piece of irony on Seltzer's part). But in the infrared of his darkroom, a hellish hue that recalls the stylised figure of Damien in the aforementioned opening credits, Jennings develops his photographs of Father Brennan outside the embassy that contain a strange anomaly: a shadowy line that intersects with his head and body. Later, when he develops his photos of the Father at the rugby match, Jennings traces his finger over the line, chillingly punctuated by Goldsmith's violins in a high-pitched descending glissando. Another omen? Or another coincidence?

2.12 Jennings uncovering a conspiracy in his darkroom.

For the subplot of a photographer capturing a conspiracy in the making through the lens of his camera, Seltzer has acknowledged the influence of Michelangelo Antonioni's paranoid New Wave thriller *Blow-Up* (1966), in which negatives are enlarged to reveal the almost imperceptible details behind a murder plot: 'I was very impressed by *Blow-Up*. A big fan of the French New Wave. And I loved how you could capture something in a still photograph that was indelible and not visible to the naked eye' (*The Devil's Word*, 2019).[6] One may also detect echoes of the even more paranoid *The Conversation* (Francis Ford Coppola, 1974), in which a surveillance audio tape catches a murder plot in the making, unheard by the human ear. Both these narratives channel Abraham Zapruder's infamous 8mm film of JFK's 1963 assassination used as key evidence in the Warren Commission, later the subject of endless analysis and dissection by conspiracy theorists. Such theorising replete with political subtext finds its way into the proto-Satanic panic of *The Omen*. On the side of the marvellous, may these photographs hold the clue to an actual Satanic plot, and reveal the material forms of the supernatural world under an imperfect or obscure reality that portends the characters' fates? Or on the uncanny side, could the anomalies be due to faulty camera emulsion? A defect in the camera itself?

Jennings could be seen as a carried-away conspiracy theorist for whom event, accident, coincidence has underlying significance; and when one paranoiac gets together with another, the hermeneutic paranoia doubles. Jennings is one of the press photographers invited to the house on Damien's birthday. He and Robert cross paths again in the aftermath of the nanny's suicide when Robert accidentally breaks the photographer's camera at the embassy, and offers to recompense him for it – which seems almost apposite in this context. At his cramped flat, Jennings shows Robert enlarged photographs of the nanny Holly with a shadowy line around her head and neck. 'It was a strange coincidence,' he pronounces, ironically. But when he shows him his photographs of the late Father Brennan, he observes of the last image he took of him before he died how the javelin-like line is 'more pronounced now and it's actually making contact with the body. And the rest, of course – history.' By now, we're teetering on the edges of the uncanny.

Jennings' investigations into the father's background only deepen the mystery and intrigue. Obtaining a copy of the coroner's report, he finds out that he was 'riddled with cancer' and 'high on morphine', suggesting he wasn't in full possession of his faculties when he spoke to Robert on those two occasions. He also mentions that, according to the report, the Father had a strange mark on his right thigh – three sixes – which Thorn blows up with the magnifying glass. 'Concentration camp?' tenders Robert. 'That's what I thought,' replies Jennings, 'But the biopsy says it's a birthmark.' Donner, for his part, thinks this too could be a 'terrible coincidence. If you go to any of the medical libraries, it's *incredible* the forms these birthmarks do take. So it could be this poor man, Peck [i.e. Robert], is caught up in such total insanity around him that he too goes insane' (Shay 1976: 46). Or could it be a form of stigmata, as reported in the annals of psychiatry? Or some form of branding from a Satanic coven or cult that casts doubt on the coroner's conclusions? For the record, Jennings presents a different explanation in the novelisation: that the biopsy showed "'it was literally carved into him. They didn't do that in the concentration camps. This was self-inflicted I'd suppose'" (Seltzer 1976: 124). Ergo, this is *not* a birthmark.

Thus, based on Jennings' investigations, we could build a picture of a priest-turned-Satanist-turned priest, who is running out of time and seeks forgiveness for his sins, presumably for his role in facilitating Satan's return to Earth.[7] That the repentant priest is/was embroiled in Satanism and some sort of conspiracy upon renouncing the Catholic order is seemingly confirmed later, when Robert manages to extract information from the now-repentant Father Spiletto about Damien's origins; a plot was hatched in a hospital in Rome, and Robert unwittingly became a part of it. Later, when Robert and Jennings' investigations take them to the ancient site of Megiddo, Bugenhagen asks Robert about the fate of the 'little priest', thereby confirming Father Brennan's role in a larger plan to *stop* the Antichrist. But, while the Devil is real enough for these believers, whether this has any *empirical* basis is an altogether different proposition.

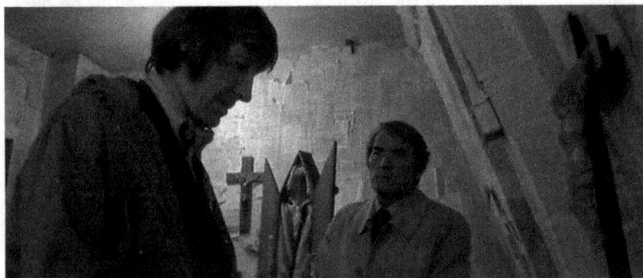

2.13 Jennings and Robert search Father Brennan's apartment for clues.

Their late-night visit to Father Brennan's slum apartment opposite a church, papered over with countless pages of the Bible and 40-odd crosses of different sizes, is like visiting the room of an inmate in an insane asylum. In rummaging through his effects beforehand, Jennings shows him the Father's diary, the diary of a madman, of Thorn's comings and goings and speaking engagements, as well as clippings from newspapers. Jennings shows Robert a cutting from the *Astrologer's Monthly* reporting an unusual astrological phenomenon that has been likened to the star of Bethlehem, which occurred five years ago on June 6. He then shows him a birth announcement for his own 'son', also five years ago on June 6. Grief-stricken, Robert is forced to make the connection – this is a film about making connections – as he confesses to this virtual stranger: 'My son is dead. I don't know whose son I'm raising.' Jennings vows to help Robert find out what's seemingly known only to the initiated few, and while Thorn declares its 'my problem', Jennings shows him a photograph of himself accidentally taken earlier in the priest's apartment that reveals another strange anomaly: a piercing black line through his own neck. Omen or coincidence?

When it comes to the adjacent genres between the uncanny and marvellous, we are at a tipping point in the narrative. Brennan's prediction about Kathy being with child, and then losing the child, is, I submit, the most alarming 'coincidence' in the narrative, and the most difficult to explain away. How could the Father possibly know? In balancing the different possibilities, it is helpful to remember Sherlock Holmes' axiom that 'When you have eliminated all which is impossible, then whatever remains, however improbable, must be the truth'. Thus, was he privy to information apropos of a pseudo-Satanic conspiracy, i.e. confidential reports from Kathy's psychiatrist or GP? And did he have knowledge that Mrs Baylock would help bring about Kathy's miscarriage? Or was it, as we like to say, a lucky guess? Confronted with circumstantial evidence and the possibility of a *human* conspiracy, Robert second-guesses his thoughts and actions. What makes his descent so hard to watch is that he is aware to varying degrees of his break with reality. This hits on the distinction sometimes made between the monomaniac, who might be aware of his own fixation, and the patient with the more specific *idée fixe*, who might not.

SEARCH FOR THE TRUTH

The final act of *The Omen* is a frantic mystery-detective thriller which centres around Robert's – and Jennings' – quest for the truth about Damien's lineage. This begins in Rome, at the centre of the conspiracy, where his son – and Damien – was born. But on arrival they learn that the hospital burned down five years ago and all the birth records have been destroyed. However, they learn from a sister in the rebuilt hospital that Father Spiletto survived the fire, and resides at the *Ill Monastero di San Domenico* in Frosinone, a town and *comune* in Lazio, 75 kilometres outside of Rome.

But when they encounter the fire-ravaged, disfigured Father, he is in a catatonic stupor; he is the half-blind seer seemingly cursed with cosmic knowledge. There's something quite Dantean about his descent into Hell – a hell on earth – for seeking out this unholy knowledge and power and for abandoning the teachings of Christ.[8] Father Spiletto's punishment almost seems like a form of poetic justice, as he wrestles with Purgatory in the confines of the monastery, begging for forgiveness and praying for entry into Heaven. On the stone floor can be found inscriptions of '666' and other markings that designate the hooded monk. Wracked with remorse and shrinking from the outside world, it is clear that for Spiletto, Satan is a real entity with real power for causing evil and havoc. But as in the Aboriginal Australian superstition of pointing the bone, could it could be that he has brought a curse upon himself, through his own suggestibility or paranoia? Robert demands that he reveal the identity of Damien's mother, and as the church bell tolls portentously he uses his non-afflicted arm to scrawl 'Cervet- ' in charcoal on the stone floor, which the attending monk takes as 'Cerveteri'; an old Etruscan cemetery, now in ruins.

Arriving at the cemetery at dusk, what Robert and Jennings find further fuels narrative ambiguity. Scaling an imposing iron-spiked fence, they find a headstone with the name Maria Scianna, dated June 6, presumably 1971, and next to it the headstone of Bambino Scianna, an infant boy, carrying the same date. But when they remove the cement block from the first grave they find the skeletal remains of a jackal (cf. Father Brennan: 'It's mother was ja-'), and here the 'Ave Satani' cue underscores the demonic significance. Although Jennings senses danger, Robert is adamant they open the other grave, clinging on to the hope, however remote, 'if it's an animal too … then maybe my child … is alive

2.14 *Robert interrogates a disfigured Father Spiletto.*

somewhere'. But confirming his worst fears, they find the skeletal remains of a baby, with its skull perforated. Goldsmith's score punctuates this moment with full force, to Robert's tortured judgements: 'They murdered him. They murdered him as soon as he was born. Murderers. Murderers.' While in *Rosemary's Baby*, Adrian/Andrew's conception – the union of a human mother and the Beast – was fairly straightforward, in *The Omen* the mind boggles at the specifics of conception – that's of course assuming it occurred at all.

Robert doesn't have time to ponder these revelations as he and Jennings become aware of a pack of Rottweilers guarding the graveyard. While in the original screenplay they were not devil-dogs but devil-hoofed figures or suchlike, we cannot categorically affirm that these dogs are spectral or demonic in origin. Making good use of a Gothic, Hammer-like set designed by Carmen Dillon (who won an Academy Award for her work on Laurence Olivier's *Hamlet*, 1948), Donner's camera prowls through the trees to take in the canines' point of view, so that while the scene has a very supernatural quality, it is not necessarily so. Despite the mounting threat, Robert must return the lid to the grave – his murdered son's grave. To not do so would be a desecration. And when they are attacked by the dogs, Goldsmith's adrenalin-pumping score takes the scene to almost delirious heights. Robert gets painfully caught on the spiked fence; Jennings, who makes it over, tries to free him. They barely make it out of the godforsaken place alive.

Donner afterwards stages Kathy's demise in an open-ended manner that *could* be a case of misadventure. Just before, Robert phones Kathy at the hospital and urges her to leave for Rome as soon as possible, without explanation. He obviously fears for her safety. But

2. 15 Robert and Jennings search for answers at the Etruscan cemetery.

as she struggles to lift the nightgown over her head, Kathy sees an indistinct reflection in the window through the gossamer. She turns around, her face a diaphanous picture of terror, as Mrs Baylock suddenly appears like a phantom. The effect is deliciously Gothic. Donner then alternates with close-ups and zooms of their faces and eyes, before showing Mrs Baylock advancing towards her (and the camera). In the next instant, Kathy is seen hurtling through the air, issuing a terrifying scream. This is intercut with an optical point of view shot of her hurtling downward. She lands inside an ambulance on a stretcher. The doors fly open to reveal her bloodied face; it's excessive, with a whiff of gallows humour. Donner has submitted that the nanny surprises Kathy as the hospital, and she *throws herself* out of the window. True, we don't actually *see* Mrs Baylock pushing her. But this may be taking the uncanny explanation too far for most viewers.

As a baleful Mary Poppins, enterprisingly sent by 'the agency', Mrs Baylock remains a conundrum in the film.[9] She appears out of nowhere on the Thorns' doorstep. Only in the novelisation do we learn that she aided and abetted Father Spiletto and Father Tassone (Father Brennan in the film). Not only does she belong to a Jamesian Gothic school of stories about mentally suspect governesses or nannies (e.g. *The Innocents*; *The Chalk Garden*, Ronald Neame, 1964; *The Nanny*, Seth Holt, 1965), but she also recalls the ice-cold housekeeper Mrs Danvers (Judith Anderson) who plots against the second Mrs de Winter (Joan Fontaine) in Alfred Hitchcock's *Rebecca* (Scahill 2012: 99). There is a scene in *Rebecca* which even anticipates Kathy's/Lee Remick's fate: Mrs Danvers, hovering over her new mistress at the high window of the Manderley mansion, tries to goad her into 'suicide' by self-defenestration. Carol L. Fry (2008: 120) describes Mrs Baylock as a 'shield for the child', seemingly 'part of the vast cult conspiracy, the shadowy

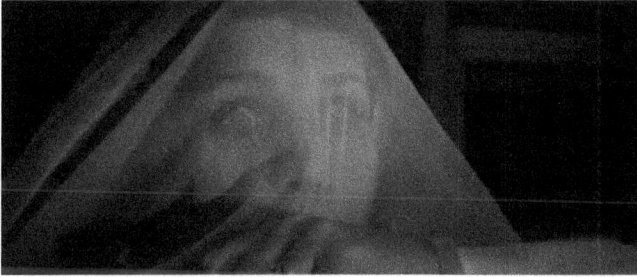

2.16 Portrait of Gothic terror.

Others, established to take care of him – and created by the scriptwriter to inspire paranoia in the audience'. She defies Robert's order to get rid of the Rottweiler that she has brought into the house as a companion – and servant? – for Damien. Bugenhagen later tells Robert that she is an 'apostate of Satan' and will die before permitting his destruction. But could she be merely a nanny after all, protecting her young charge from Robert's insanely murderous intentions? At least Donner entertained this possibility. For all that, it's much harder to explain away her part in Kathy's demise.

From his accommodation in Rome, Robert receives a phone call with the earth-shattering news that his wife has just died in an accident. Did we ever see the strong, stalwart Peck cry on screen before now? Well, he does here, and as emoted by the actor from the more is less school of acting, the character's grief is palpable. It would be no exaggeration to say that what we're witnessing here is the unravelling of post-war hegemonic masculinity. No doubt Robert blames himself. But could it be that he is looking for someone else to blame? In terms of his psychopathology, we can imagine him redirecting the hate he feels toward himself, for failing in his duty to protect his vulnerable wife, to Damien himself: the scapegoat for his failure and inadequacy. To atone for his own insurmountable grief, set the world in balance, the child must die.

By this stage, his *idée fixe* is determining every thought and action, reaffirmed later when Robert is able to recall the name of the man Father Brennan told him to see. As if springing from a deep well within his unconscious that is symptomatic of the idea Janet theorised develops 'autonomously, involuntarily, and subconsciously' (Heim & Bühler 2006: 113), he tells Jennings, 'It's Bugenhagen.' Jennings intimates that he was an exorcist he has read about. 'That was his name,' Robert affirms, 'and I remember the poem.' And as the camera tracks slowly to a tight close-up of his grief-stricken face, Robert recites the poem word perfect, after hearing it only once from the Father. It is as if the poem was always there, inside his subconscious, merely awaiting the right cue for retrieval. Robert adds with quiet resolve: 'Kathy is dead. I want Damien to die, too.'

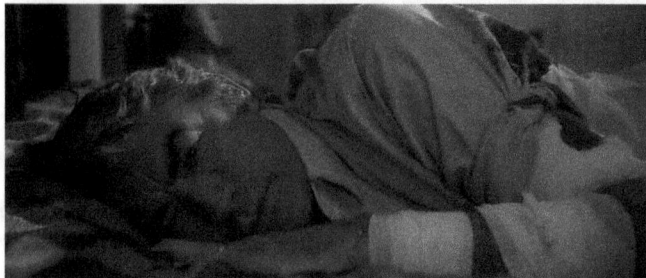

2.17 Robert overwhelmed by grief.

'IS THERE PROOF?'

At the site of the ancient city of Megiddo under excavation, Bugenhagen delivers his special instructions to Thorn on how to kill the Antichrist. As colourfully portrayed by the portly Leo McKern, the archaeologist-exorcist vaguely recalls Jesuit priest-archaeologist Father Merrin (Max von Sydow) of *The Exorcist*, who faces off with the demon Pazuzu at a dig in the famous Iraq prologue.[10] He sends Jennings away as he makes his endowment, for his instructions are for Thorn and Thorn alone. These are a set of seven consecrated knives (called the seven knives of Megiddo in *The Final Conflict*). As he arranges the knives upright in the pattern of a crucifix, he expounds:

It must be done on hallowed ground. A church. His blood must be spilled on the altar of God. This first knife is most important. It extinguishes physical life and forms the centre of the cross. The subsequent placings extinguish spiritual life, and should radiate outward like this. This is not a human child. Make no mistake.

Robert grabs one of the knives, half-miming the action of thrusting and inserting, non-committally.

2.18 *Bugenhagen (Leo McKern) delivers his special instructions on how to kill the Antichrist.*

Even at this late stage, Robert asks, 'Is there proof?' Bugenhagen points to the birthmark, the sequence of sixes, shared by all the apostles of Satan. Robert claims that he has never seen such a mark, having bathed him countless times. 'If it is not visible on the body,' Bugenhagen apprises, 'it will be beneath the hair. Remove it. You must be devoid of pity.' The exhaustive search for the Devil's or Witches' mark on the accused's body was of course standard witch-hunting procedure in the purges of early modern Europe and colonial America. The mark, states the *Encyclopedia of Witchcraft and Demonology* (1974: 26), 'was supposed to be made of Satan's teeth, tongue or claw, and in some cases it was actually the "Devil's claw". It might be in the shape of a spider, a dormouse or "the likeness of a hare", and according to some early medieval authorities it could be compared with the imprint of a cloven hoof.' But the notion of three '666s' applied to the human body is, as far as I can tell, largely Seltzer's invention, as inspired by the passage from Revelation chapter 13, verse 18: that the number of a beast is 'six hundred threescore and six'. After *The Omen*, the numerical marker became much more embedded within demonology and popular culture.

However, Robert's encounter with Bugenhagen undermines not strengthens his resolve. In a bustling street, he tells Jennings with utter disbelief: 'I'm the one that's supposed to kill him. These are *knives*. He wants me to *stab him!* Wants me to murder a child!' Jennings exclaims, 'It's not a child!', in no doubt of what 'needs' to be done. But Robert second guesses himself as he desperately clings on to reason and sanity: 'How can he *know* that? Maybe he's wrong. It's insane! I won't have anything to do with murdering a little boy. He's not responsible, I won't do it!' as he throws – spurns – the knives which land at an active construction site. 'Well, if you don't do it,' resolves Jennings, 'I will,' as he goes over to retrieve the knives. But as Jennings does so, a workman gets out of his truck and 'accidentally' touches the handbrake. The truck rolls back and a pane of glass slides off the back and cleanly decapitates him; Jennings' head rolls in Grand Guignol fashion. Using overlapping editing and slow motion – to stretch out real time for shocking impact – Donner stages his 'execution' from multiple angles. Jennings' head lands in front of a shattered piece of glass; lifeless eyes 'staring' at its final reflection, the final moment of truth.

2.19 Robert refuses to see.

In *The Omen*, eyes here convey the truth, but always under an imperfect vision of reality. When Robert sees Jennings' decapitated body, he turns around and covers his eyes, refuses to face the truth – refuses to see. He is like Oedipus, cursed by the gods, wanting to gouge out his own eyes because of the horror he has inadvertently caused (Oedipus: 'What good were eyes to me?/ Nothing I could see could bring me joy'). One may surmise that he feels responsible for the deaths of Jennings, Kathy and others, and feels more duty-bound than ever to rid the world of the Antichrist. But like Hamlet, we sense his mind twisting and turning, agonising over what he thinks he must do. Flying back to England, he carries the bundle of daggers on his lap. The camera slowly tracks away from a profile of his face to reveal a forlorn and even tragic figure; Robert is the only passenger on the private jet. All this seems like the proverbial calm before the storm.

But before he can follow through, he must find the last piece of evidence – the final, incontrovertible proof. When Robert arrives at the mansion late at night, Goldsmith's eerie chants – redolent of a black mass à la *Rosemary's Baby* – seem to spill over into the diegetic world. After trapping in the cellar the Rottweiler that Mrs Baylock has been keeping against his wishes, Robert goes over to the marital bed; a piano rendition of the love theme over shrill, dissonant strings conveys sorrow and unease. He then takes a pair of hair-cutting shears and, while Mrs Baylock sleeps in the next room, proceeds to cut Damien's hair under the flicker of the fireplace. As he cuts away, the film slows down ever so slightly, and we go from a close-up to an extreme close-up to the microscopic. Shining a lamp on the centre of his scalp Robert finds a clover leaf-like arrangement of sixes – a birthmark? Or an initiation from an errant sect? His face is suffused in the light of the lamp, and it would seem he has seen the terrible light. Or has he only been blinded?

And then Mrs Baylock seems to burst into the frame, screaming 'No!', leading to a ferocious free-for-all accompanied by Goldsmith's shrieking choir. The woman hits, scratches, bites, and claws as Robert tries to shake her off. Damien is first transfixed on the bed. But when she cries out 'Run! Run!' he cowers behind a chair – exactly like a terrified, innocent child might. He doesn't even attempt to assist his beloved nursemaid. In the drawn-out scrimmage, Donner crosscuts to the howling dog trying to get out of the cellar.[11] Robert finally despatches the nanny with a kitchen utensil, then bundles Damien into the car and zooms out of the estate, ignoring a policeman's attempt to intercept him. It's a 'possible diplomatic incident' and a race against the end times.

As Damien is dragged kicking and screaming from the car to the church, he is, for all intents and appearances, an innocent child – one, perhaps, who's greatly misunderstood and whose rumours about his wickedness have been greatly exaggerated. This uncertainty further underscores how the child is the site of extremely conflicting adult attitudes towards children; the Romantic/Rousseauian child, born in a state of innocence until corrupted by civilisation and culture, or the Calvinist/Puritan child, born into a state of wickedness. As much as the Romantic construction of the child appears to hold sway in contemporary Western culture, the relationship between these opposing ideologies of childhood is 'not only one of competition, or of coexistence, but of codependence' (Schober 2004: 7). And as a reversible child figure, Damien is *both*.

The penultimate scene re-enacts and reworks the Binding of Isaac. As related in chapter 22 of the Book of Genesis, Abraham follows the commandment from God to sacrifice his only son Isaac on the altar, before an angel messenger stops him and presents him with a ram to sacrifice instead. Through his would-be sacrifice, Abraham demonstrates his fear of God. But what of this half-beast, half-jackal child? Is it to be slaughtered like an animal? In the funk of the moment, is Robert acknowledging that he fears God – and Satan (the one receiving meaning from the other)? Has he been converted to a renewed belief in Catholicism and the Devil? Peck, we know, was uncomfortable with performing the filicidal act on screen. In fact, the makers of *The Omen* had hesitated about sending the script to Peck, whose troubled son had shot himself in June 1975. The devastated father had agonised over what he could have done to prevent it (Fishgall 2002: 286-7). Perhaps the idea of killing one's own child was too close to home for the actor. What we do know is that Peck worried how this act might be detrimental to his screen image, impelling Donner to come up with a way to make the scene more open-ended, or at least palatable.

2.20 'God help me!'

Enacted over a very discordant rendering of the love theme, a bloodied, wretched Robert drags the little boy down the church aisle and onto the altar, holding him down with one hand. As he is about to drive in the dagger that will extinguish physical life, Damien cries, unnervingly, 'No! Please, Daddy, no! No, Daddy no!' For Williams (2014: 119), this 'may be the cries of a child who does not understand his true story', supporting the child-as-villain conception. Or it may be the cries of a child who's frightened out of his wits! Robert cries, 'God help me!' as the police arrive on the scene not a moment too late, shouting 'Police! Drop! Drop, or I'll fire!' Cut to a close-up of the powder load and bullet discharging from a policeman's handgun, achieved using a high-speed camera and intense lighting of the bullet in slow motion. The screen fills with grainy white.

CHAPTER 3: UNTIL MAN EXISTS NO MORE

But the film does not end here. Not quite.

In the coda, we witness a military-style funeral service accompanied by news cameramen, with two – not three – caskets on display. The place is presumably Washington DC, Arlington, Virginia or suchlike (actually the American Military Cemetery, part of Brookwood Cemetery, 45km southwest of London). The clergyman concludes the service with an 'Amen'. Three shots are fired as the military funeral dirge 'Taps' is played on the bugle. Servicemen fold the American flag and the mourners begin to disperse. Then a trench-coated man goes over to the standing figure in an overcoat and says, 'Excuse me, Mr President. When you're ready to leave, your car is right over there.' He answers, 'In a moment.' The First Lady and President of the United States both have their backs to the camera, with the caskets visible in the centre of the frame. The camera then cranes down to reveal a third person standing between them: Damien. He then turns his head around, stares directly into camera, and breaks into grin, as 'Ave Satani' begins to play. This fades out to the white-on-black quotation from scripture before the closing credits: 'Here is wisdom. Let him that hath understanding count the number of the Beast: for it is the number of a man; and his number is 666. – Book of Revelation Ch 13 verse 18.' The end.

It is a bravura closing shot, and one of the unequivocally knowing moments of the film. After all the serious goings-on up to this point, Damien has just broken the fourth wall; he – and Donner – is winking at the audience. One suspects that Donner was agreeing with his prospective critics that what we've just witnessed is hokum. After directing the scene, Donner recalled the negative reaction: '[E]verybody said, "Don't do that, you'll ruin the movie. He's laughing at the movie." Everybody fought me. [But] I felt what the smiling boy was saying was, "Is this all true? Has this been a put-on? Am I the Devil?"' (Christie 2010: 89). Indeed, it's almost as if he was pulling the rug out from under the movie. For Scahill (2012: 99), '[Damien's] direct glance at the camera and devious smirk suggest a [sic] untoward knowledge and a recognition of the audience, desirous of further carnage'. But is he smiling at us maleficently? Or innocently?

3.1 Damien breaks the fourth wall at the end of The Omen.

As an empty cipher, with few defining features, with precious little to actually *say* in the movie, the little boy becomes the repository of adult anxiety and desires, on which the characters – and the carefully 'primed' audience – can ascribe demonic significance. While Goldsmith's score is hardly subtle here, seemingly closing off alternative meanings, the celebrated shot demonstrates the truth to James R. Kincaid's assertion that we, as the audience, manage this 'double act'

> by switching the costume we put on the child: idealized angels are made possible by matching devils. And it's simple economy to use the same body for both parts: the dream child becomes the demon. The dark side of our desire is projected outward onto the demon child, who occupies a variety of figures ranging from naughty to satanic, all of them alien to us, resistant, disobedient. This child is always running away from us, forcing us into a chase at least as alluring as the stasis offered by the perfectly adorable child.

> But they are the same child. The monster is the logical continuation of the cherub …
> (Kincaid 1998: 140-141)

Damien is the ravenous wolf in sheep's clothing; the Antichrist as false prophet. The effect is very Jamesian, underscoring tensions between Romantic and Calvinist/Puritan ideologies of childhood.

Yet the ironic ending to *The Omen* was not without precedent. In William March's 1954 novel *The Bad Seed*, sociopathic child Rhoda Penmark survives her mother's attempt to kill her, and she lives to kill again. Like Robert Thorn, Mrs Christine Penmark dies trying to rid humanity of a lusus naturae, which is to say that this is another narrative that ascribes evil in the child to genetic rather than environmental factors. Rhoda also survives in the Broadway play, where – much like Damien – she 'fiendishly winks at the audience afterward, making them complicit in her killings' (Kincaid 1998: 158). Contrast this with Mervyn LeRoy's 1956 film version, which revises the fate of the evil child in the opposite direction. To appease the Motion Picture Production Code, the film metes out its own form of poetic justice when the little miscreant is struck down by God's lighting. (This seems like the next best thing to the electric chair.) Yet Rhoda or, rather, the actress playing her, is resurrected in a fashion during the curtain call. When 'Miss Patty McCormack as Rhoda' does an ironic curtsey to camera, she breaks – not unlike Damien – the fourth wall. She is then given a good ol' spanking by her screen mother, Nancy Kelly/Christine ('And as for you …'), in a half-joking attempt to reassert parental discipline over the forces of heredity, and no doubt intended to provide some measure of reassurance to the audience.

Yet *The Omen* was to originally end with *three* caskets shown – those of Kathy, Robert *and* Damien. Due to pressure not from censors but because of feedback from Hollywood executives at 20th Century Fox, Alan Ladd Jr. had Donner go to the Shepperton backlot to shoot a new ending where the devil-child lives. This was in the spring of 1976. While this is widely accepted as a last-minute addition, a version of this ending does appear in an add-on to Seltzer's revised screenplay dated 26 September 1975, while the film was still undergoing principal photography.[12] *The Omen*'s ending was also rigorously tested on preview audiences, allowing for some eleventh-hour fine-tuning, as the film's director explained: 'In one [variation] the kid didn't turn at all, in another he turned but didn't look directly into the camera. There was no reaction. But when he smiled, the audiences went wild. I can't explain it. It just seems to work' (Arnold 1976: E2). It caused such a jolt that many 'seem to believe they're looking at a second, reincarnated child' (Arnold 1976: E2), which Donner acknowledged was a misinterpretation.

Not only would this surprise ending leave the door open for sequels, but it would have far-reaching implications for the meanings we take away from the film. For if Damien had died at the hands of his adoptive father, then we'd have a fairly clear-cut case of order restored. The patriarchal Establishment, after this close call, survives more or less intact. In South Africa, in fact, the film ended with Robert about to stab Damien, giving this exact impression. The fact that he lives puts him on track to fulfilling the prophecy that will undermine and eventually destroy the Establishment, from within the corridors of power.[13] The full military honours accorded to the funeral of the ambassador and his wife screams government conspiracy and cover-up.

Whether this ending is left- or right-wing in its politics and implications is hard to say. *Films and Filming* considered Damien's infiltration into the White House a 'heavyweight touch', and a 'desperate apology for any lack of evident saintliness among the political set: let us not be quick to blame them for they might be possessed by Satan' (Gow 1976: 30). For *Monthly Film Bulletin* it was a 'banal bicentennial coup, as the evil finally lands himself in the White House' (Combs 1976: 171). Roger Ebert (1976: 63) quipped that it would 'leave you thinking that Nixon wasn't half bad'. *Film Illustrated*'s critic, looking back on the trilogy that anti-climaxed with *The Final Conflict*, observed: 'When the Satanic stood side by side with the US President at the conclusion of Richard Donner's first innings, audiences cried aloud, "Nixon!" and the film's dark pessimism seemed perfectly in key with the post-Watergate paranoia that rocked American politics' (Whitman 1981: 5). In casting Damien in Nixon's image, threatening to tear down the government, such responses aren't left or right, necessarily. For even staunch Republicans, Nixon had gone too far and his conduct was unconscionable, putting a stain on the party and politics more generally.

For some, though, *The Omen* carried a paranoid and pernicious right-wing agenda. In his thoughtful exegesis for *Cineaste*, Duncan Leigh Cooper saw the coda as deeply flawed, in that it runs counter to the logical thrust of the narrative. Yet he acknowledged how the ending hit home the film's real theme, if we strip away the supernatural trappings of the narrative, that

> … the kind of power which really counts today is political. As portrayed in *The Omen*, the real menace to humanity lies not in Damien's supernatural power, but in his possible future rise to high political office. In the same way, not demonic force but state power thwarts Thorn in his attempt to save us from this menace. Thus, *The Omen* is an exceedingly political film, and its politics are reactionary in the extreme. (Cooper 1976-77: 47).

For Cooper, *The Omen* played into the kind of right-wing paranoia that gives rise to conspiracy theories used to legitimate the actions of individuals to stop the subversion of America's 'free' institutions. But he also noted that that the film does not act as a safety valve for that paranoia – as many other horror/disaster films of the period do through repeated exposure – but, rather, serves to increase it (Cooper 1976: 46). Thus, *The Omen* cannot be properly labelled proto-Reaganite or Reaganite entertainment, at least not in the way influential critic Andrew Britton (1986) defines it, which is not only ideologically conservative, reactionary, unchallenging but, above all, *reassuring*.

The Omen, according to Robin Wood in his initial critique, was far more revolutionary in its implications. 'Inevitably, a reading of the film tends to become a reading *against* it; one longs to reverse all its terms. Yet the rigour with which the implications are seen through to their logical conclusion is exemplary: the systematic annihilation of *all* the "Establishment" characters as the Devil prepares to take over the world' (Wood 1976: 12). The implication of reading against the grain implies that the 'norms by which we have lived must be destroyed and a radically new form of organisation (political, social, ideological, sexual) be constructed; the alternative is "the end of the world"' (Wood 1976: 12). As he acknowledges, the contemporary American horror film has seldom confronted the implications of this 'reorganisation', but it is hard to tell whether this reflects the radical critic's wish fulfilment or that of the filmmakers'. 'What our civilization needs,' Wood (1976: 12) concludes, 'is a cinematic William Blake capable of daring to imagine the Devil as hero,' which, as I discuss in Chapter 4, is what is precisely attempted in *The Final Conflict*.

In the updated edition of *Hollywood From Vietnam to Reagan ... and Beyond*, Wood shows how he had moved on somewhat in his thinking on the film when he writes:

> The translation of the film into Blakean terms is not in fact that difficult: the devil-child is its implicit hero, whose systematic destruction of the bourgeois Establishment the audience follows with a secret relish. *The Omen* would make no sense in a society that was not prepared to enjoy and surreptitiously condone the working out of its own destruction. (Wood 2003: 80)

Wood's references to Blake here seem particularly apt: in *The Marriage of Heaven and Hell* (1794), the English Romantic poet presented a vision of the imminent apocalypse that resonated with the events of the French and American revolutions. Invoking the Book of Revelation, he wrote that the 'ancient tradition of the world will be consumed by fire at the end of six thousand years is true, as I have heard from Hell' (Blake 1975; xxi-xxii). 'Without contraries,' declared he, 'there is no progression' (Blake 1975: xvi), as he sought to overturn such entrenched terms or oppositions as love/hate, good/ evil, heaven/hell, and attraction/repulsion. *The Omen* is likewise a film that revels in the instability of its oppositions, e.g. delusion/reality, sanity/insanity, good/evil, Christ/Antichrist, cross/inverted cross, conservative/radical, and so on. The three sixes, a monk expounds, signify the Diabolical Trinity: the Devil, Antichrist and false prophet. This is, of course, a mockery of the Holy Trinity: Father, Son and Holy Ghost.[14] One instantly thinks of the three faces of Dante's Satan as a mockery of the Trinity. Despite the film's cavalier treatment of religion and belief, this oppositional mindset is central to the creed of Satanists: 'Whatever Christianity does, uses and preaches, they do, use and preach the opposite' (Stanford 1996: 237).

Yet Wood (2003: 80) sounds a note of dissatisfaction when he writes that *The Omen*, along with *The Texas Chainsaw Massacre*, can only envision an ideology of despair, instead of offering 'constructive radical alternatives'. For this reason, it falls short of Blake's radical vision of revolution, moral revisionism and 'apocalypse.' Rather, the film is driven by a nihilistic wish to witness the end of the world, implying a subtext about the generation of post-1960s radicals (including counterculture) not so much overthrowing but annihilating the Establishment altogether, without putting anything in its place; a vision that is dystopian, if not apocalyptic. For all his trenchant criticisms of contemporary American society in his writings, Mark Jancovich (1992: 97) writes that the Marxist-inclined Wood 'fails to identify a specific basis for resistance, or even a constructive, radical alternative of his own', reminding us of cultural critic Raymond Williams' (1989: 209) sage advice on political activism: that it is in 'making hope practical, rather than despair convincing, that we must resume and change and extend our campaigns'.

Any Marxist ideological critique of *The Omen* would of course need to delve deeper into the intersections between politics and class. To this writer's knowledge, only Andrew Scahill takes up this issue at any length, in seeing Damien's rise to power across the films as inextricably linked to class insurrection, his followers acting as his servants. In the shocking suicide of the nanny Holly on the occasion of Damien's fifth birthday party, for example, Scahill (2012: 96) sees something quite subversive in the way 'Bourgeois whiteness is upended by the technology of class subjugation, and necessitated by the invisible labor of the economic underclass.' One could equally claim that the film dramatizes the *threat* of class insurrection, which serves as a warning to conservatives to do whatever it takes to preserve the status quo. To be fair, Scahill acknowledges how these unstable configurations of class, race and childhood in the film can be construed as both radical and reactionary. Holly, Father Brennan and Mrs Baylock could be counted among the underclass; so too can Jennings, whose unlikely teaming up with an ambassador suggests an uncomfortable mixing of the classes. In any case, the apocalyptic, radical vision that so impressed Wood may not be so radical after all: merely the replacement of one established order with another.

Couched in less nihilistic but no less disturbing terms, *The Omen* could be promising a New World Order (certainly this is the case in *The Final Conflict*) – but, needless to say, this is no paradise or New Jerusalem, in the Blakeian sense. Playing on Cold War fears, it invokes an alien political system, founded on tyranny and repression. But perhaps worse than a world taken over by Communists is one taken over by Satanists – or perhaps they are essentially one and the same. 'For many evangelical Christians,' explains Carrol L. Fry (2008: 12), 'the New World Order is similar to the Communist menace of the 1950s, seen as a malignant and ungodly force in our society that not only threatens individual freedom but subverts Christianity. The more extreme believers see it as a conspiracy of the Antichrist,' further fuelling fears about paranoia and conspiracy and the fear of the Other. Accordingly, Nikolas Schreck (2001: 180) dismisses *The Omen* as 'concealed Christian propaganda masquerading as a mainstream movie', tailored to the American religious right. He writes that it 'moved a central tenet of the theocratic agenda to extremist born-again Christianity into the minds of its viewers, signalling a shift in American popular consciousness toward the rise of cultural Reaganism' (2001: 181). Throughout his two terms as US president, Ronald Reagan appropriated Satanic and apocalyptic rhetoric when he framed the arms race as the battle between good and evil, and Communism as a story of temptation and the fall (Poole 2009: 169). Reagan, notoriously, referred to the former Soviet Union as the 'evil empire'.

Upon its release, critics found *The Omen*'s subtext on the corrupt state of contemporary American politics hard to miss. Yet at the time, Donner declared,

'There was never any intention of making a movie whose emphasis was religious or philosophical. There are bound to be deeper implications for some people, but *The Omen* is basically a genre picture' (Arnold 1976: E2). As aforementioned, the much-too-grounded director never took the film's premise seriously (nor, for that matter, did Seltzer or star Peck), even while he called on his actors to play it straight. (For the record, Donner categorically rejected that there was ever a curse on the production.) And it would seem that he is having the last laugh. For this is a movie calculated in its effects and scares, with an ending based on audience research, and a massive pre-sell campaign that cynically tapped into premillennial fears. *The Omen* may be read as an affirmation of conservative Christian values – or the opposite. As Robin Wood knew, viewers take to the film what they bring to it.[15]

Thus far in my study, I have come to *The Omen* on its own terms. In the next chapter, I consider the religious and political implications of the continuing story of Damien's rise – and fall – in the two sequels, which offer some revisions to the first film, not to mention foundational American myths.

CHAPTER 4: SATANIC ANTI-HERO

Buoyed by the box-office success of *The Omen*, producer Harvey Bernhard disclosed
to *Variety* on September 1, 1976 that he and 20th Century Fox would be embarking
on three other sequels, continuing the story of Damien the Antichrist as an eleven-year
old, a teen, and a man aged between 35-40 (anon. b 1976: 3). Only two more theatrical
sequels were eventually produced, and, some time after the fact, a television film. (There
would also be a remake and a television series, cancelled after only one season.) *Damien:
Omen II* was made for almost twice the budget as *The Omen*. Richard Donner, tied up
with Warners' highly-anticipated *Superman: The Movie*, was unable to direct. Bernhard
then turned to English director Mike Hodges, responsible for the crime drama *Get
Carter* (1971) and sci-fi thriller *The Terminal Man* (1972). Hodges also co-wrote the
screenplay with Stanley Mann, after David Seltzer declined to be involved. However,
Hodges was fired early on in production, apparently because of his slow working
methods which were threatening to put the film over budget and behind schedule. By
some accounts, Hodges wanted to craft a more thoughtful, 'artistic' picture that would
stand the test of time. What the studio and Bernhard wanted was a no-nonsense sequel;
Hodges was duly replaced by American journeyman Don Taylor.

The film received mostly negative reviews, with one critic sniping that 'Something should
be done about the boy promptly before he does something really awful – like setting up
another sequel' (Castell 1978: 23). *Cinefatastique*'s Bill Kelley (1978: 64), however, thought
it a superior sequel, 'a taut, lean reworking of the most interesting ideas from the first
film'. In retrospect, it stands alongside *Jaws 2* (Jeannot Szwarc, 1978) and *Dawn of the
Dead* (George A. Romero, 1978) as one of the better horror sequels of the 1970s;
a mostly worthy successor, filling the difficult middle act. *Damien: Omen II* grossed US
$26.5 million at the box office, less than half of the original.

The opening in Jerusalem picks up after the events of the first film. Bugenhagen (Leo
McKern, again) drives his jeep with urgency through the old city of Acre in Israel
to meet with his archaeologist friend Michael Morgan (Ian Hendry). He shows him
the headline in *The Times* that reads 'US Ambassador and Wife Buried Together in
Washington'. It is dated Tuesday, January 6, 1976, thereby confirming the implied timeline
of the original film. Telling him he has seen the face of Damien as the Antichrist on

the recently excavated Yigael's wall, Bugenhagen asks Michael to deliver a coffer with the daggers (no explanation is given on how these were returned to his possession so swiftly) and a letter addressed to Robert Thorn's industrialist brother, Richard. Bugenhagen takes the disbelieving Michael to the archaeological site of Yigael's wall. This is marked by the appearance of a raven, à la Poe's raven, which takes over from the Rottweiler in *The Omen* in the symbolism stakes. Upon showing him Damien's likeness on the wall, with serpents instead of hair, Satanic forces appear to be awakened and both are buried alive within the subterranean structure, as Bugenhagen prays for salvation.

It is seven years later, which places *Damien: Omen II* in the near future. Damien (Jonathan Scott-Taylor) is 12 years old and living with his uncle Richard (William Holden, who had turned down the role of Robert Thorn) and his younger wife Ann (Lee Grant) in their Chicago mansion. He is being raised with his same-age cousin Mark (Lucas Donat), a child from Richard's deceased first wife. This, of course, overturns – and waters down – the political implications of the first film, namely that Damien would be raised in the White House by the President and First Lady. As Bernhard sought to explain this away, 'He [Richard] couldn't be there for his brother's funeral, so the President came – it shows the power of the family' (Shay 1978: 53).

4.1 The impressive Jonathan Scott-Taylor as Damien on the cusp of manhood in Damien: Omen II.

In shifting the backdrop from international diplomacy to corporate America, *Damien: Omen II* enlarges upon the apocalyptic paranoia of the first film with fears about overpopulation and food scarcity. In 1968, Stanford University Professor Paul R. Erlich published his bestselling *The Population Bomb* which made dire predictions about the near future. 'Each year food production in undeveloped countries falls a bit further behind burgeoning population growth, and people go to bed a little bit hungrier,' he wrote. 'While there are temporary or local reversals of this trend, it now seems inevitable that it will continue to its logical conclusion: mass starvation' (Erlich 1971: 17). In April 1970, a day after the first Earth Day celebration, the *New York Times* issued a warning to humanity: 'Man must stop pollution and conserve his resources, not merely to enhance existence but to save the race from intolerable deterioration and possible extinction' (Christofferson 2004: 7). The impact of the ongoing energy crisis in the 1970s recession seemed to simultaneously mark the end of the post-war American boom and the start of America's decline as an economic superpower.

As CEO of a multinational corporation, Richard is assisted by rising executive Paul Buher (Robert Foxworth), who is looking for the company to expand its interests in energy and electronics into farming in Third-World countries – or, as Paul puts it in his crass fashion, 'Our profitable future, aside from energy, lies also in famine.' His scheme involves buying up land from these countries, and producing and controlling their food supply, which may be seen as an indirect reprisal against the Middle East for the 1973 oil crisis. It also smacks of colonialist and paternalistic intentions. Paul is opposed at every turn by aging president Bill Atherton (Lew Ayres), who thinks the scheme unethical. Amid concerns about population outstripping food supply, the company that can control the world's food supply controls the world. Bill is disposed of by an unfortunate 'accident' during an ice hockey game at the Thorns' Wisconsin lake house, leaving Paul unobstructed. Paul is a ruthless Machiavellian operator plotting his way up the corporate ladder, with a little help from his Satanic friends.

But *Damien: Omen II*'s prime concern is with Damien's coming of age. As played by British newcomer Jonathan Scott-Taylor, Damien is prepossessing, intense and compelling. When we first meet him, he is in his cadet uniform, about to leave with his cousin for the military academy. In a carefully composed shot – one of Hodges' surviving contributions to the finished film – the camera zooms in on Damien as he walks towards the bonfire a gardener is tending on the Thorn estate. The shift toward a telephoto range both enlarges the image and flattens its planes together so that it appears he is walking through the flames – a suggestive piece of imagery!

Damien is positioned as 'on the cusp'. Or as Paul Buher lectures the boy: 'A boy's thirteenth birthday is considered by many as the beginning of puberty, of manhood. Many cultures have initiation rites. You'll be initiated, too, Damien. Yes, the timing is coming for you to put aside childish things and face up to who you are. A great moment, Damien. Surely you must be feeling it?' 'I think so,' he replies. 'I'm not sure. But I feel that something's happening to me. Is going to happen.' It's safe to say that this is not your stock-standard adolescent *sturm und drang*. Paul assures him about these 'suspicions of destiny' shared by all great men, like his uncle, Bill and himself. Paul, we now suspect, is an emissary of Satan, as is fellow orphan and platoon sergeant at the academy Neff (Lance Henriksen). The implication is that Damien will be groomed for big business, before he enters into politics. Earlier, after Damien confesses to Paul that he doesn't know anything about his role at the company, Paul replies, 'Well, you should. You should know everything about the Thorn business; after all, it'll be yours one day.' 'And Mark's,' Damien corrects, unaware of his destiny.

Whereas *The Omen* was about efforts to protect the Antichrist from harm and destruction, *Damien: Omen II* is concerned with efforts to educate him about his destiny so that he can protect himself. The film is the crucial second act in a male *Bildungsroman*, dealing with the Antichrist's formative years and most unusual passage from innocence to experience (Schober 2004: 19). When Neff catches Damien drawing attention to himself in the classroom by his preternatural knowledge of historical dates and names, he tells him to read his Bible, specifically, the Book of Revelation. 'For you,' Neff says, 'it is just that, a book of revelation. For you, about you. Read it, thirteenth chapter. Read, learn, understand.' For dramatic tension, Taylor crosscuts between the military band going through its graduation parade drill and Damien's reading from Revelation, as he learns the truth about himself. When he discovers the cluster of sixes on his scalp using a hand-mirror in the bathroom, the knowledge it brings is tantamount to a fall. Overwhelmed, he runs away against a background of trees in the fall, and, not unlike Jesus in the Garden of Gethsemane, appeals to Satan the Father, 'Why me, why me?' Then 'in a strangely elegiac note, after Damien has recovered from the shock of his initial self-realisation, the camera tracks slowly round the two buglers playing taps [sic] in the darkened hall of the academy' (Combs 1978: 238).

At this turning point in the narrative, Damien ceases to be innocent villain. But even with the cell structure of jackal, one wonders if his good impulses could counteract the bad, given the right influence. When it comes to Mark, the film shows us how he may 'not be entirely evil, that a torturous struggle of good versus evil is taking place within his soul' (Schober 2004: 21). 'I love you, Mark, you're like my brother,' cries Damien, during their confrontation in the snow-covered woods of the lake house. We have no reason to doubt his sincerity. This comes after Mark finds out that Damien is the Beast, born of a jackal. 'Yes,' Damien admits with renewed pride. 'Born in the image of the greatest power in the world. The Desolate One. Desolate because his greatness was taken from him and he was cast down. But he has risen, Mark, in me.' Upon his surrogate brother's refusal to join him in his reign, Damien wills an artery wall to burst in his brain, perhaps recalling Cain's killing of his brother Abel in the Book of Genesis. And while the killing is a kind of initiation, a rite of passage into evil and violence, it is attended by an anguished scream. As before, when he runs from the truth about himself, Damien seems in this moment 'lost'. Yes, this is a devil with a conscience, and he damn near enlists our sympathy.

Echoing Cassandra from Greek myth, the people around Richard who utter prophecies about Damien are cursed to be disbelieved, before meeting their obligatory death. This includes freelance journalist Joan Hart (Elizabeth Shepherd), who, wearing a gaudy red coat, is attacked by a raven, before being run over by a truck;[16] and Thorn museum curator Dr Charles Warren (Nicholas Pryor) who is impaled by a train boxcar after he receives the crate containing the daggers and letter sent by Bugenhagen. Ann refuses to countenance such a belief, until we realise that she too is an emissary of Satan, the Whore of Babylon foretold in Revelation. In the basement of the museum, she stabs Richard with the daggers before he can carry out his own plan, proclaiming, 'Here is [sic] your daggers. I've always belonged to him.' But, as also foretold, Damien wills the boiler in the adjacent room to explode, setting fire to the room and burning her alive.[17]

In a nod and a wink to the original film, Damien descends the steps of the Thorn family museum, and as he gazes triumphantly off into the distance the police department arrives. A limousine awaits. The frame freezes on a close-up of his face. The film ends with the paranoia-inducing quotation: 'For such are false prophets, deceitful workers, transforming themselves into the apostles of Christ (II COR. 11: 13).' With no one left to root for, we are rooting for Damien.

Conceived and promoted as the final chapter in a trilogy, *The Final Conflict* (or *Omen III: The Final Conflict* in some markets) was the feature film debut of English director Graham Baker, who had graduated from television commercials. It was based on a literate screenplay by Andrew Birkin, whose award-winning script for BBC mini-series *The Lost Boys* (1978) about Scottish writer J.M Barrie and his relationship with the Llewelyn Davies boys had earned high praise. Although he would never direct a sequel, Donner served as executive producer on the film. But this final chapter yielded somewhat less at the box-office than *Damien: Omen II*, and the reviews were even more withering. *Variety* thought it was 'the funniest one yet' (*Har.* 1981: 20). A lone voice was Sheila Benson (1981: C11) of *The Los Angeles Times*, who praised Barker for rounding off the 'gaudy trilogy with the most surprising qualities possible: intelligence and elegant visual style'. Today, the more measured assessment of *Cinefantastique* seems about right: 'The series final is not a total waste of time and talent, only it is too tame in spots where all hell (literally) should have broken loose' (Glover 1981: 50). It is marred by an ending which must be the greatest 'non-ending' in series history.

If *The Omen* is a slow-burn suspenser, and *Damien: Omen II* a much more visceral exercise, then *The Final Conflict* is a religio-philosophical tract. Goldsmith switches gears for the music score, turning away from dark Gregorian chants to grand operatic themes, while going for a more cosmic-numinous quality marking the Second Coming of Christ. Whereas Satan was front and centre in the first two instalments, *The Final Conflict* is much more Manichean in its outlook, dramatizing the age-old struggle between God and Satan, the Christ and the Antichrist. 'The power of evil is no longer in the hands of a child,' declared the theatrical poster's tagline; and, after a two-year search, up-and-coming New Zealand actor Sam Neill was cast in the role of Damien Thorn. Neill seems right for the part. Though evil and seductive, he presents more of a rounded and credible figure. However, in accounting for why the movie failed to click with audiences, it was perhaps inevitable that evil embodied in an adult would be less riveting than in a child or adolescent.

Set 20 years after the last film, Damien is 32, nearing the age when Jesus Christ was crucified, which is to say Birkin pulls out all the stops with parallels between the two messiahs from different camps. England is the main backdrop, for out of the 'angel isle' Christ shall return and do battle with the Beast. But in order to make the story work

4.2 *All grown up. Sam Neill as Damien Thorn in the anticlimactic* The Final Conflict.

the makers have jumped ahead of the timescale of the first two films. In a recap of his career by British TV journalist Kate Reynolds (Lisa Harrow) on her talk show program, we learn that Damien has been compared to the late John F. Kennedy, that he graduated at Yale University before coming to Oxford as a Rhodes Scholar, took over his uncle's business, Thorn Industries, in 1971, before being appointed Ambassador to Great Britain, the same position held by his adoptive father, and President of the United Nations Youth Council. Earlier, Damien tells the unscrupulous US President in the Oval Office that he can only hold the post of Ambassador for two years because he intends to run for the Senate in '84. Neither Harvey Bernhard nor Birkin seemed to have cared much about this awkward retconning.

Much more politically engaged than the first two instalments, *The Final Conflict* is a film calibrated to Jimmy Carter's purported pessimism. During a private screening, Damien watches with his Thorn Industries associates a commercial that promotes the company as a panacea to the social and economic ills of the era. For 'true believers' this reads like a cataloguing of events in the Great Tribulation, as the narrator of the commercial makes clear: 'The economic crisis of the past decade has brought inflation, famine, and chaos to every corner of the globe. Some label it the Great Recession. Others are calling it Armageddon, that final upheaval of the world foretold by the prophets of old. But amid all the pessimism, one voice rings out if faith in the future. Thorn, the world's leading light in building a new tomorrow.' Damien dismisses the advert as 'trite, rhetorical, cliched and inane'. Satan's spawn is now indistinguishable from the corporate capitalist.

In his economic and political machinations, the charismatic Damien is hellbent on assuming the United States' highest office. He is, in short, Machiavelli's prince, the multimillionaire head of a corporation masquerading as a Good Samaritan. The pseudo-liberal extolling the virtues of youth and defending the values of the current generation. 'The most important task I have,' he speechifies on UK television, 'is to help young people gain a more prominent role in world affairs than the one we currently afford them, or rather deny them', adding that we ply youth 'with our values, we indoctrinate them with our mediocrity' that is tantamount to brainwashing. Suffice it to say, Damien is using his influential position as United Nations Youth Council President to brainwash youth as well as adults into his vision of world domination, a New World Order. His rise to power, however, is threatened on two fronts: by the Second Coming of Christ, as foretold in the Book of Revelation which has received astronomical confirmation in the star alignment of the trinity; and the attempts by a posse of priests from a Dominican monastery (the same one that sheltered the disgraced Father Spiletto in *The Omen*, although the location is peculiarly identified as Subiaco, not Frosinone as in the original)[18] to assassinate him with the sacred daggers retrieved from the ruins of the Thorn Museum in *Damien: Omen II*.

Neil Gerlach (2011: 1041) reads Damien's trajectory in the trilogy as a dark inversion of the American monomythic hero, as 'not an everyman, but a product of American wealth and power. He does not come from outside of dominant institutions, but rather, moves easily within the structures of democratic capitalist society.' As written by Birkin, the adult Damien takes after the reinterpreted Lucifer of Milton's epic poem *Paradise Lost* (1667): a fallen angel rebelling against his maker, 'a sublime human figure' and a 'ready vehicle for oppositionist ideology' (Schock 1993: 451-2). This 'misreading' of Milton recasts Lucifer's fall from grace as the 'fortunate fall' (or *felix culpa*). Edward Simon (2017: 275), interestingly, sees something very American in the depiction here of the Devil: 'he is a confidence man, advertiser, rebel, partisan of liberty, and faker at the same time, self-made, a rugged individualist setting out into the wilderness to make his own world anew'. Damien, without question, expresses these Luciferian faces of the

American character; he is narcissistic, ruthless, decadent, dangerous and entitled. And as an attractive figure of evil, whose unique mission is to make the world over in his image, whose sense of destiny is a perversion of Manifest Destiny, Damien is American exceptionalism at its worst.

When Blake reappropriated this half-sympathetic image of Satan from *Paradise Lost* for *The Marriage of Heaven and Hell*, he wrote: 'The reason Milton wrote in fetters when he wrote of Angels & God, and at liberty when of Devils & Hell, is because he was a true Poet and of the Devil's party without knowing it' (1975: xvii). For Blake, Heaven or 'good' is lifeless and repressive, while Hell or 'evil' is vital and liberating. In addition to the Miltonic overtones of Lucifer in exile, there are Blakeian inversions aplenty in Damien's diatribes against Christianity in his Satanic chapel that houses a 'back-to-front' representation of Christ on the cross after an actual German carving, circa fourteenth century:

> Oh, my father, Lord of silence, supreme god of desolation, who mankind reviles yet aches to embrace, strengthen my purpose to save the world from a second ordeal in Jesus Christ and his grubby, mundane creed. Two thousand years have been enough. Show man instead loneliness, the purity of evil, the paradise of pain. What perverted imagination has fed man the lie that hell festers in the bowels of the earth? There is only one hell, the leaden monotony of human existence. There is only one heaven, the ecstasy of my father's kingdom …

> We were both created in man's image. But while you were born of an impotent god, I was conceived of a jackal …

True to the sadomasochistic creed implied in his acquired moniker, Damien clutches the Crown of Thorns with both hands, then disappears into the shadows as blood – his blood – seeps from Christ's forehead. It's a highly perverse image that may be understood as a Blakeian contrary of Christ and Antichrist as two opposing but necessary forces. As he pontificates to imminent lover Kate, 'Most people confuse evil with their own trivial lusts and perversions. Now true evil is as pure as innocence.' Read through Blake's invented mythology, Damien is Orc from *America a Prophecy* (1793) rebelling against the tyranny of reason and morality embodied by Urizen: '[a] Blasphemous Demon, Antichrist, hater of Dignities/Lover of wild rebellion and transgresser of God's law' (Blake 2008: 89). By extension, Gerlach (2011: 1041) views Damien's rant as a 'Nietzschean attack on the fundamental moral principles that underlie ideas of Western civilization, [in which] the Antichrist comes to represent our fears about what we are becoming in late modernity'.

In the history repeats schema of Birkin's narrative, Damien's sermon to the Disciples of the Watch in the canyon mirrors Christ's Sermon on the Mount. What is more, his command to them to slaughter every male infant born before March 24 re-enacts King Herod's Massacre of the Innocents to eradicate the Christ Child. Along these lines, Kate Reynolds, whom Damien refers to as 'the Barbara Walters of British Television', can be read as a Mary Magdalene figure who tempts his 'humanity' and threatens to derail his mission and purpose. When his private secretary and advisor, Harvey Dean (Don Gordon), tries to warn him that she is dangerous, Damien angrily replies, 'I decide who is dangerous.' Ironically, he fails to heed the ill-omen.

After bungled attempts by the band of brothers led by Father DeCarlo (Rossano Brazzi) to despatch the Antichrist, DeCarlo convinces Kate, whose adolescent son Peter (Barnaby Holm) has fallen under Damien's evil influence,[19] to help lay a trap. With Peter in tow, Kate drives Damien to a darkened, ruined English abbey. But when De Carlo leaps out to stab him with one of the daggers, Damien uses Peter as a human shield; Peter dies. After almost throttling De Carlo to death, Damien is stabbed in the back by Kate with one of the remaining daggers. Letting out a cosmic scream, Damien staggers to where the altar of the abbey would have been. He is met with ethereal light – and the triumphant image of Jesus Christ. As he falls to the knees, Damien utters the dying words, 'Nazarene, you have won … nothing,' his resistance to Christ and his preordained fate shown to be futile. In this regard, *The Final Conflict* revises the implication of the first two films that the Antichrist can only be slain with all seven daggers.

The film ends with not one, but two Biblical quotations, the second taken from the Book of Revelation, chapter 20, verse 4: 'And God shall wipe away all tears from their eyes; and there shall be no more death, neither sorrow, not crying, neither shall there be any more pain: for the former things are passed away.' This proclamation notably does not include resurrection for the misused boy Peter. The ending was singled out for ridicule, with one critic calling it 'laughingly reminiscent of something like *King of Kings*

[Nicholas Ray, 1961]' (Ward 1981: 312); another a 'stampede into religiosity worthy of De Mille' (Combs 1981: 198). It is a most unsatisfying finale, yet suggestive of how more uplifting treatments of spirituality in the cinema, as in the case of the underrated *Resurrection* (Daniel Petrie, 1980) released the previous year, are a hard sell.

Receiving its premiere on the Fox Network in 1991, the Canadian-made *Omen IV: The Awakening* seems more like a mutant offspring to the franchise. It was the last in the series to be produced by Harvey Bernhard, who died in 2014. He also co-wrote the script, which revolves around eight-year-old Delia (Asia Vieira), who is adopted as a baby by Virginian congressman Gene York (Michael Woods) and his unable-to-conceive attorney wife Karen (Faye Grant) from an orphanage run by Catholic nuns. Like Robert Thorn, York is from a politically illustrious family and is on the way up. In fact, much of *Omen IV* is a re-tread of *The Omen*, with matching scenes and situations (including a series of bizarre, violent deaths, toned down for TV), dialogue, and a variation on the original twist ending that brings us full circle. We learn that Delia is not only Damien's daughter but that she carries the seed of her evil twin brother, which has been transplanted into her adoptive mother; like the unwitting mother of *Rosemary's Baby*, Karen gives birth to the new Antichrist. While many evangelists have viewed the 'occult' practices of New Agers as in league with the Devil, Delia feels threatened by crystal healing and the like – when her New Age nanny tricks her into having a Kirlian photograph taken at a psychic fair it reveals a negative life force. In retaliation, Delia causes the fair to go up in a hellish conflagration. 'In one unimaginative swoop,' remarked a reviewer from Australia (where the telefilm received a limited theatrical release), '*Omen IV: The Awakening* obliterates any lingering traces of glamour left by its three successful predecessors. It's hard to believe that anyone could reduce the usually reliable entertainment factors of demons among us and world apocalypse to snooze level but this does it' (Lowing 1991: 100).

CONCLUSION

After polarising critics on its release in 1976, *The Omen*'s critical reputation continued to suffer over the years. In *The Fifty Worst Films of All Time* (1979), Harry and Michael Medved listed *The Omen* as their most recent 'worst' entry, alongside the likes of *Ivan the Terrible, Part 1* (Sergei Eisenstein, 1944), *Valley of the Dolls* (Mark Robson, 1967), *Zabriskie Point* (Michelangelo Antonioni, 1970) and *The Last Movie* (Dennis Hopper, 1971). The film enthusiast brothers levelled much of their criticism at the acting, writing and direction. Gregory Peck's performance, which now seems a model of restraint and is imbued with riveting undercurrents of guilt, was an easy target: 'His delivery is punctuated by so many lengthy and "dramatic" pauses that at times we are left to wonder whether the great actor has fallen asleep. In this role, Mr. Peck expresses every emotion simply by raising his left eyebrow [!]' (Medved & Medved 1979: 173). Nor did *The Omen* fare well in later genre surveys. For example, Peter Nicholls (1984: 139) was dismissive: 'This glossy, glazed attempt to rework the traditional horror picture … for a respectable audience was commercially successful, but as a film it does not amount to much.' In contrast, Phil Hardy (1984: 317) in his horror encyclopaedia was able to muster some praise for the film: 'Though sometimes rather slowed down by its production values, *The Omen* is an atmospherically shot …accomplished entertainment.'

Since then, *The Omen* has undergone a critical reappraisal and is widely regarded as a classic of the horror genre, if perhaps a minor one. It figures in personal selections by film critics and so-called experts; recently, *Empire* ranked it #21 in a list of the 50 best horror movies of all time, while *Time Out* ranked it #25 in a list of 100 all-time best. In 2002, the American Film Institute also placed it #81 on its list of the 100 most thrilling American films. On Rotten Tomatoes it has an average rating of 86% based on 50 reviews. According to the review aggregator site's consensus: '*The Omen* eschews an excess of gore in favor of ramping up the suspense – and creates an enduring, dread-soaked classic along the way.' It of course birthed a franchise of dwindling quality. As a measure of the film's pop culture impact, the name 'Damien' has since become a byword for an evil child, ripe for parody in *Mad Magazine*, *South Park*, *Saturday Night Live*, and the long-running BBC comedy, *Only Fools and Horses*. The 2019 Amazon/BBC television series *Good Omens*, based on the 1990 novel by Terry Pratchett and Neil

Gaiman, depicts a comic mix-up at a convent hospital in which the Antichrist is put into the custody of a quaint Oxfordshire couple instead of an American ambassador and his wife. However, the 'excellent' name Damien for the (wrong) baby is rejected in favour of the 'old English name' Warlock! But all this, along with rumours surrounding a curse on the movie, has arguably deterred serious critical analysis, something which I have sought to address in this monograph.

As I have been at pains to argue, the question of Damien's moral agency is a central source of ambiguity in the film, one largely forgotten in the wake of the sequels. This was something that director Richard Donner (who died of heart failure in July 2021, drawing a chorus of tributes) and writer David Seltzer very consciously built into the fabric of the narrative. Indeed, in the absence of overt Satanic imagery, one might go as far as to say that the entire narrative of *The Omen* is couched in the subjunctive mood, negotiating a Jamesian tension between the explicable and inexplicable, or (in Todorovian terms) the uncanny and marvellous. This throws up questions that do not have easy answers, namely: is Robert Thorn the victim of paranoia or an actual conspiracy? Is Damien the son of the Devil? Is the belief in the Devil grounded in delusion or empirical reality? Could the deaths in the movie be explained in rational terms? (The 'accidental' manner of the deaths in *The Omen* and its sequels seems to have influenced the *Final Destination* [2001-2011] franchise.) For Todorov, this uncertainty lies at the crux of the fantastic. Revisiting *The Omen* with fresh eyes, one can expect a multi-layered exercise in terror and suspense.

Not to downplay its international appeal, *The Omen* is fuelled by an American strain of paranoia, which may be regarded as the *raison d'être* for the narrative. Further factoring into the ambiguity, this includes paranoia about: the end times; government and conspiracy; child-rearing (especially if one strips away the thin layer of Satanism); and paranoia about real or imagined threats to the hardening right-wing Establishment from liberal and post-countercultural forces of the 1970s. With its slippery politics, unresolved contradictions, religious and moral panic (which would spiral into the Satanic ritual abuse panic of the 1980s and 1990s), *The Omen* has proven appeal for both liberals and conservatives, and as such the perfect echo chamber for cultural political ideology and the wildest conspiracy theory. By the time we arrive at the sequels, *Damien: Omen II* and *The Final Conflict*, the darker side to American exceptionalism is exposed in the explicit linking of Satanism to Machiavellian discourses of big business and government. Damien, who starts out as an unreadable, cipher child, grows into a 'terrible' adolescent, and emerges as a half-sympathetic Satanic anti-hero. The trilogy, however, would end on a stunningly anticlimactic note.

Although *The Omen* was a motion picture for the times, the apocalyptic theme itself is timeless – and amenable. As British literary critic Frank Kermode wrote in his 1967 magnum opus *The Sense of an Ending*:

> The great majority of interpretations of Apocalypse assume that the End is pretty near. Consequently the historical allegory is always having to be revised; time discredits it. And this is important. Apocalypse can be disconfirmed without being discredited. This is part of its extraordinary resilience. It can also absorb changing interests, rival apocalypses such as Sibylline writings. It is patient of change and of historiographical sophistications. It allows itself to be diffused, blended with other varieties of fiction … and yet it can survive in very naïve forms. (Kermode 2000: 8-9)

And so, perhaps inevitably, Fox greenlit a remake released on the 6th day of the 6th month 2006, thirty years to the day after the UK release of the original. *The Omen: 666* offers an update of postmillennial fears that includes references to 9/11, natural disasters and the 2003 Columbia Shuttle disaster. As directed without distinction by John Moore and transcribed (one can hardly say 'written') by Dan McDermott, the film is a less subtle and ambiguous affair. So similar was McDermott's script to David Seltzer's original screenplay that the Writer's Guild of America denied him a screen credit. Seltzer was awarded full credit instead, despite the fact that he had no involvement in the production. This time round we have Liev Schreiber as Robert Thorn and Julia Stiles as his long-suffering wife Kathy. Both are unremarkable, as is the rest of the cast, including Seamus Davey-Fitzpatrick in the key role of Damien. The only interesting piece of casting is Mia Farrow as Mrs Baylock. As Rosemary Woodhouse, Farrow was the progenitor of the devil-child, the one that 'started it all'. It is thus fitting that she would one day play Damien's guardian.

There may be no better testament to *The Omen*'s artistry and power than to compare it to this by-the-numbers remake, which is as devoid of atmosphere and *gravitas* as it is of Donner's craftsmanship and style. The recreated scenes – like the nanny's suicide,

Damien's tantrum in the car, the animals going berserk at the zoo, the canine attack at the cemetery – fall flat. And Marco Beltrami's score is singularly lacking, despite utilising some of Goldsmith's original cues. Even though the box-office was strong, most critics regarded it as inferior to the original. Writing for *Rolling Stone*, Peter Travers (2006) opined, 'Not since Gus Van Sant inexplicably directed a shot-by-shot remake of Hitchcock's *Psycho* has a thriller been copied with so little point or impact'. (Bizarrely, Roger Ebert gave the 'thumbs up' to this sorry rehash.) To quote Final Girl Sidney Prescott in *Scream 4* (Wes Craven, 2011) on the first rule about remakes: 'Don't fuck with the original.'

Remember … you have been warned.

NOTES

1. In addition to *Rosemary's Baby* and *The Omen*, these Satanic-themed films include, inter alia, *The Witches* (Cyril Frankel, 1966), *The Devil Rides Out* (Terence Fisher, 1968), *The Blood on Satan's Claw* (Piers Haggard, 1971), *The Brotherhood of Satan* (Bernhard McEveety, 1971), *The Wicker Man* (Robin Hardy, 1974), *Race with the Devil* (Jack Starrett, 1975), *Look What's Happened to Rosemary's Baby* (Sam O'Steen, 1976, made for TV), *To the Devil … a Daughter* (Peter Sykes, 1976), and, of course, *Damien: Omen II* (Don Taylor, 1978).

2. In his entry on Donner for *The New Biographical Dictionary of Film*, David Thomson (2016: 296) gives one of his outrageously pithy dismissals: 'Mr. Donner has made several of the most successful and least interesting films of his age. And one doubts it's over yet.'

3. Unless quoting directly from *The Omen* or its sequels, all quotations to the Holy Bible in the text are from the King James Version.

4. Remick refused to fall to the floor, so Donner had to improvise. He had her 'fall' horizontally against a wall, using a dolly and turntable. Sardines painted to look like goldfish, plastic water and glass, a rug and palm tree were stuck to the wall. As the proud director says of the finished shot in the featurette *666: The Omen Revealed* (2000): 'It became a conversation piece – how the hell did they do that?'

5. As a fundamental principle of editing described by the Soviet filmmaker and theorist Lev Kuleshov (1899-1970), the Kuleshov effect states that 'the meaning produced by joining two shots together transcends the visual information contained in each individual shot. In other words, the meaning of a sequence of shots is more than the sum of its parts' (Pramaggiore & Wallis 2005: 162).

6. This was spoofed in Mel Brooks's affectionate Hitchcockian comedy, *High Anxiety* (1977), where a black-and-white photograph is blown up to astronomical dimensions to expose a fiendish frame-up.

7. In the novelisation, the Irish cleric is imagined differently, as the Portuguese-born Edgardo Emilio Tassone, raised in a monastery before becoming a priest, and spending his early years in Africa as a missionary. We are told he fled Africa when his affair with a tribal boy was exposed. Under Father Spilletto's evil tutelage, the pederastic priest renounced Christ and the Church and turned to the worshipping

of Satan; revelling in his new faith around carnal pleasures and the blaspheming of God; and becoming part of a global network of Satanists bent on creating fear and turmoil. Most significantly, we learn that he was responsible for the murder of Robert's son, bashing his head in with a stone, as he did to the jackal. But after receiving his malignant tumour diagnosis, Tassone is driven by a need for repentance, forgiveness (Seltzer 1976: 93-98). Such backstory can only be treated as deep background on Father Brennan, to enhance our understanding of what Seltzer had in mind.

8. On these Dantean aspects of Father Spiletto's depiction, I am grateful to Dr Matthew Jarvis for his insights, as host for my online talk: 'Be Warned! From the Eternal Sea He Rises: Paranoia, Politics, and *The Omen*', Spooky Evenings, academic e-event, Wesleyan Nebraska University, Lincoln, 15 October 2021, https://www.youtube.com/watch?v=GHQwlnY44nM

9. Seltzer has revealed that Mrs Baylock's name derives from scripture, after the figures of Balak and Balaam. As recounted in the Book of Numbers, chapters 22-24, Balak King of Moab induces the magician and prophet Balaam to curse the Jewish people, because he feels threatened by their numbers and influence. But God intervenes before Balaam can deliver his curse to the Jews and instructs him to bless them instead. Mrs Baylock is much more suggestive of Balak alone, as an enemy of the Jewish people, than as a conflation of these two figures. Yet, like Balaam, she is ambiguous, which partly revolves around the question of whether she represents a blessing or a curse.

10. Author and screenwriter of *The Exorcist*, William Peter Blatty, modelled the character of Father Merrin on real-life French Jesuit-cum-geologist-palaeontologist Teilhard du Chardin (1881-1955).

11. Carrol L. Fry (2008: 120) claims that 'On the dog's side, we see a reflection of a cross on the wall. The origin of the reflection is unclear in the film. But it rotates during the scene, perhaps suggesting the ambivalent outcome of the battle of good, the upright cross, and evil, an inverted cross.' If this was a deliberate effect, then this goes hand in hand with the previously discussed symbolism of the cross/inverted cross in the opening title sequence. More than suggesting the ambivalent outcome of good versus evil, it highlights the ambivalent nature of the narrative itself.

12. At the service, we make out a child in the company of a dignified man and his wife, and the child is, of course, Damien. He looks 'beautiful and restored, wearing a heavy bandage on his arms', as he gazes calmly down at the two caskets. After the officiating priest bestows his blessings and graces on the child, two members of the President's detail go over to the man and wife. One of them says, 'Mr, President? Your car is this way.' '[L]eft alone at the grave: Damien [is] in the custody of his new parent – flanked by Secret Service men on either side' (Seltzer 1975: 124). Fade out. The end.

13. Before *The Final Conflict* worked through the particulars of this prophecy in the now grown-up Damien, false heir to the Thorn family's fortunes and powerful connections, *The Changeling* (Peter Mendak, 1980) showed the outcome of such a 'changeling' plot. To hold on to the family inheritance, a father has murdered his sick, sequestered boy in the bathtub of an old mansion and replaced him with a healthy one. The unwitting imposter in this plot is now an elder statesman in the US Senate (an aging Melvyn Douglas). Meanwhile, the mansion that once belonged to the statesman is haunted by the ghost of the murdered boy now seeking retribution.

14. Or in the grave, portentous tones of the narrator in the TV spot: 'For everything known, there is something unknown. For every blessing there is a curse. For everything holy there is something unholy. For every evil there is an omen'.

15. This is notably true of *The Exorcist* with its similarly ambivalent ending. In his introduction to the 25th anniversary edition of *The Exorcist*, director William Friedkin states: 'Most people take out of *The Exorcist* what they bring to it. If you believe that the world is a dark and evil place, *The Exorcist* will reinforce that. If you believe there is a force for good that combats and eventually triumphs over evil, then you'll be taking out of the film what we tried to put into it.'

16. Joan Hart's demise vaguely recalls the avian attack on the schoolchildren in Alfred Hitchcock's *The Birds* (1963), which comes as no surprise, given that Ray Berwick, who trained the birds in that film, was also hired to train the ravens for *Damien: Omen II*. As for her striking red garment, original director Mike Hodges wanted her to evoke the mysterious woman in red in the paintings of Edvard Munch (lest we missed the significance, there is a Munch exhibition at the Thorn Museum).

17. As her final moments are colourfully rendered in the novelisation: 'Joyous in her flaming death, like some demonic Joan of Arc, she lifted her face toward the heavens and cried out, 'Damien! *Damien! DAMIEN!*' (Howard 1978/1985: 191).

18. It appears Birkin conflated details from Seltzer's novelisation of *The Omen* (in which the site of the monastery is identified as Subiaco) with the film when he wrote the screenplay for *The Final Conflict*.

19. One may glean a pederastic subtext in the film that pathologises homosexuality. Of the unseemly relationship between Damien and Peter, Mark Sutton noted in his astute review that the boy is 'significantly played by Barnaby Holm, who looked so right in the role of the oldest son in *The Lost Boys*, the BBC drama [written by Birkin] about James Barrie (in which the writer was represented as a tragic, non-practising paedophile)'. Pederasty is figured as symptomatic of Damien's closet homosexuality. In his satanic chapel, Damien 'fondles and caresses' the statue of the crucified Christ, leading Sutton (1981: 46) to conclude of the ending: 'Cashing in on current paranoia about the destruction of all civilised values, the film features a stunningly literal and ludicrous Born-Again finale in which a brightly radiant Christ stands triumphant over the fallen body of Damien, faggot Antichrist.' For an unpacking of the queer meanings in the series, see Scahill (2012).

BIBLIOGRAPHY

666: The Omen Revealed [documentary] Produced and directed by J.M. Kenny. 20th Century Fox, United States, 2000.

AFI (2002) 'AFI's 100 Years ... 100 Thrills: The 100 Most Thrilling American Films.' Available at https://www.afi.com/afis-100-years-100-thrills/ [accessed 30 January 2022].

AFI/Catalog. Entry on *The Omen* (1976). Available at https://catalog.afi.com/Catalog/moviedetails/55833 [accessed 11 April 2020].

Albanese, C.L. (1992) *America: Religions and Religion*. Belmont, California: Wadsworth Publishing Company.

Alighieri, D. (2012) *The Divine Comedy: Inferno, Purgatorio, Paradiso*, trans. R. Kirkpatrick. London: Penguin.

Anon. a (1972) 'The Occult: A Substitute Faith', TIME Magazine. Vol. 99, Issue 25. 19 June. 62-68.

Anon. b (1976) '*Omen* Hits $40-Mil U.S. Gross; Bernhard Maps Three Sequels', *Variety*. Vol. 284, September. 1. 3+

Anon. c (1976) '*The Omen* Sensational Seller in Bookstores', *Boxoffice*. Vol. 109, 19 July. 12.

Anon. d (1976) 'Theology Laurels *Omen*', *Variety*. Vol. 283, No. 6. 16 June. 6.

Anon. e (1976) 'Catholic B (as in Berate) to "Omen" for Mismash Dogma,' *Variety*, Vol. 283. 7 July. 5.

Appelbaum, R. (1976) 'Making and Selling *The Omen*', *Filmmakers Newsletter*. Sept. 30-36.

Arnold, G. (1976) 'Richard Donner: Heeding *The Omen*', *Washington Post*. 25 July. E1-2.

Benson, S. (1981) '*Final Conflict* Ends *Omen* Saga', *Los Angeles Times*. 21 March. C11.

Blake, W. (1975) *The Marriage of Heaven and Hell*. Oxford: Oxford University Press.

Blake, W. (2008) *Blake's Poetry and Designs: Illuminated Works Other Writings Criticism*, selected and ed. by Mary Lynn Johnson and John E. Grant. 2nd ed. New York and London: Norton.

Boyer, P (2008) 'The Evangelical Resurgence in 1970s American Protestantism', in B.J. Schulman and J.E. Zelizer (eds) *Rightward Bound: Making America Conservative in the 1970s*. Cambridge, MA; London: Harvard University Press. 29-51.

Britton, A. (1986) 'Blissing Out: The Politics of Reaganite Entertainment', *Movie*. Vol. 31/32. Winter. 1-42.

Büssing, S. (1987) *Aliens in the Home: The Child in Horror Fiction*. New York: Greenwood Press.

Carty, T.J. (2004) *A Catholic in the White House? Religion, Politics, and John F. Kennedy's Presidential Campaign*. Houndmills, Basingstoke: Palgrave Macmillan.

Castell, D. (1976) 'Richard Donner & *The Omen*', *Films Illustrated*. Vol. 6. Nov. 102-103.

Castell, D. (1978) Review of *Damien: Omen II*, *Films Illustrated*. Vol. 8. 22-23.

Christie, J. (2010) *You're the Director ... You Figure it Out: The Life and Times of Richard Donner*. Duncan, Oklahoma: BearManor Media.

Christofferson, B. (2004) *The Man from Clear Lake: Earth Day Founder Senator Gaylord Nelson*. Wisconsin: University of Wisconsin Press.

Cobley, P. (2002) '"Justifiable Paranoia": The Politics of Conspiracy in 1970s American Film', in X. Mendick (ed.) *Shocking Cinema of the Seventies*. Hereford: NOIR Publishing. 74-87.

Combs, R. (1976) Review of *The Omen*, *Monthly Film Bulletin*. Vol. 43. Aug. 170-171.

Combs, R. (1978) Review of *Damien: Omen II*, *Monthly Film Bulletin*. Vol. 45, No. 539. Dec. 237-238.

Combs, R. (1981) Review of *The Final Conflict*, *Monthly Film Bulletin*. Vol. 48. Oct 198.

Cooper, D.L. (1976-1977) Review of *The Omen*, *Cineaste*. Vol. 7, No. 4. 46-47.

Counts, K.B. (1976) Review of *The Omen*, *Cinefantastique*. Vol. 5, No. 2. 27.

Crist, J. (1976) Review of *The Omen*, *Saturday Review*. July 24. 42-3.

Dean, D. (1976) Review of *The Omen*, *Films in Review*. Vol. 27. Aug/Sept. 440.

The Devil's Word [short film] Produced and directed by Edwin Samuelson. Samuelson Studios/Shout! Factory, United States, 2019. Special feature on *The Omen Collection: Deluxe Edition*, Blu-ray.

Ebert, R. (1976) 'A Wicked Little Devil on a Tricycle', *Chicago-Sun Times*. 28 June. 63.

Encyclopedia of Witchcraft and Demonology: An Illustrated Encyclopedia of Witches, Demons, Sorcerers and their Present Day Counterparts. (1974) Intro. Hans Holzer. London: Octopus Books.

Eder, R. (1976) 'The Screen: *The Omen* is Nobody's Baby', *New York Times*. 26 June. 12.

Elliott, J.K. (1993) *The Apocryphal New Testament: A Collection of Apocryphal Christian Literature in the English Translation*. Oxford: Oxford University Press.

Empire Online (2021) 'The 50 Best Horror Films.' 4 August. Available at https://www.empireonline.com/movies/features/best-horror-movies/ [accessed 30 January 2022].

Erlich, P.R. (1970) *The Population Bomb*. New York: Ballantine.

Finler, J.R. (2003) *The Hollywood Story*. London: Wallflower Press.

Fishgall, G. (2002) *Gregory Peck: A Biography*. New York: Scribner.

Fry, C.L. (2008) *Cinema of the Occult: New Age, Satanism, Wicca, and Spiritualism in Film*. Bethlehem: Lehigh University Press.

Gerlach, N. (2011) 'The Antichrist as Anti-Monomyth: *The Omen* Films as Social Critique', *The Journal of Popular Culture*. Vol. 44, No. 5. 1027-1046.

Gilliatt, P. (1976) 'The Current Cinema: Diabolism Sells', *The New Yorker*. 19 June. 85-87.

Girard, R. (2001) *I See Satan Fall Like Lightning*. Maryknoll, New York: Orbis Books.

Glover, R.A. (1981) Review of *The Final Conflict*, *Cinefantastique*. Vol. 11, No. 2. 50.

Goldstein, J. (1987) *Console and Classify: the French Psychiatric Profession in the Nineteenth Century*. Cambridge: Cambridge University Press.

Gow, G. (1976) Review of *The Omen*, *Films and Filming*. Vol. 23. Nov. 30-31.

Grimes, W. (2003) 'Gregory Peck at 87; Film Roles had Moral Fiber', *New York Times*. 13 June 2003, available at https://www.nytimes.com/2003/06/13/movies/gregory-peck-is-dead-at-87-film-roles-had-moral-fiber.html [accessed 13 March 2020].

Guariento, S.M. (2019) *Light into Ink: A Critical Survey of 50 Film Novelizations*. [US]. Self-published.

Haney, L. (2005) *Gregory Peck: A Charmed Life*. London: Robson Books.

Har. (1981) Review of *The Final Conflict*, *Variety*. Vol. 302, No. 8. 25 March. 20.

Hardy, P. (1986) *The Encyclopedia of Horror Movies*. London: Octopus Books.

Heim, G. and Bühler, K-E. (2006) 'Psychological Trauma and Fixed Ideas in Pierre Janet's Conception of Dissociative Disorders', *American Journal of Psychotherapy*. Vol. 60, No. 2. 111-129.

The Holy Bible in the King James Version. (1984) Nashville: Thomas Nelson.

Howard, J. (1978/1985) *Damien: Omen II*. London: Futura.

Howard, T. (1976) Review of *The Omen*, *Christianity Today*. Vol. 20, No. 2. 6 August. 1121-1122.

Jacobs, M. (2008) 'The Conservative Struggle and the Energy Crisis', in B.J. Schulman and J.E. Zelizer (eds) *Rightward Bound: Making American Conservative in the 1970s*. Cambridge, MA: Harvard University Press. 193-209.

Jackson, K. M. (1986) *Images of Children in American Film: A Sociocultural Analysis*. Metuchen, NJ and London: Scarecrow Press.

James, H. (1998) *The Turn of the Screw and Other Stories*. Oxford and New York: Oxford University Press. (Originally published 1898.)

Jancovich, M. (1992) *Horror*. London: B.T. Batsford.

Kelley, B. (1978) Review of *Damien: Omen II*, *Cinefantastique*. Vol. 74, No. 4. 64-65.

Kermode, F. (2000) *The Sense of an Ending: Studies in the Theory of Fiction: with a New Epilogue*. New York: Oxford University Press.

Kincaid, J.R. (1998) *Erotic Innocence: The Culture of Child Molesting*. Durham, NC: Duke University Press.

Kolker, R. (2011) *A Cinema of Loneliness: Penn, Stone, Kubrick, Scorsese, Spielberg, Altman*. 4th ed. Oxford: Oxford University Press.

Kruse, K.M. and J.E. Zelizer (2019) *Fault Lines: A History of the United States Since 1974*. New York: WW. Norton & Company.

Kucharsky, D. (1976) 'The Year of the Evangelical', *Christianity Today*. Vol. 21, No. 2. October 22. 12-13.

Lassiter, M.D. (2008) 'Inventing Family Values', in B.J. Schulman and J.E. Zelizer (eds) *Rightward Bound: Making American Conservative in the 1970s*. Cambridge, MA: Harvard University Press. 13-28.

LaVey, A.S. (2005) *The Satanic Bible*. New York: Avon Books.

Levin, I. (1968) *Rosemary's Baby*. London: Pan. (Originally published 1967.)

Lowing, R. (1991). 'Bad Omen for Demon Watchers', *The Sun-Herald*. 18 August. 100.

McGill, G. (1980/1985) *The Final Conflict – Omen III*. London: Futura.

Medved, H. & M. Medved with R. Dreyfuss (1979) *The Fifty Worst Movies of All Time (and How They Got That Way)*. London, Sydney and Melbourne: Angus & Robertson.

Murf. (1976) Review of *The Omen*, *Variety*. Vol. 283, No. 5. 9 June. 23.

Murray, J.C. (1977) Review of *The Omen*, *Cinema Papers*. Vol. 11. Jan. 266-7.

Newton, M. (2020) *Rosemary's Baby*. BFI Film Classics. London: BFI/Bloomsbury.

Nicholls, P. (1984). *Fantastic Films: An Illustrated Survey*. New York: Dodd, Mead & Company.

The Omen Legacy [documentary] Produced and directed by Brent Zacky. Prometheus Entertainment/20th Century Fox, United States, 2001.

Paul VI. (2013) 'Be Strong in the Faith in Order to Stand Against the Power of Darkness.' *Humanitas*. No. 4. 435-7.

Perchaluk, E. (1976) Review of *The Omen*, *Independent Film Journal*. Vol. 78. 25 June. 13.

Pramaggiore, M. and T. Wallis (2005) *Film: A Critical Introduction*. London: Laurence King Publishing.

Poole, W.S. (2009) *Satan in America: The Devil We Know*. Lanham, Maryland: Rowman and Littlefield.

Powers, S., D.J. Rothman and S. Rothman (1996) *Hollywood's America: Social and Political Themes in Motion Pictures*. Boulder, Colorado: Westview Press.

Remembering Rosemary [documentary] Produced by Karen Stetler. Criterion Collection, United States, 2012.

Renner, K.J. (2013) 'The Apocalypse Begins at Home: The Antichrist-as-Child Film', *Frame*. Vol. 26, No. 1. May. 47-59.

Scahill, A. (2012) '"It's All for You, Damien!": Oedipal Horror and Racial Privilege in the *Omen* Series', in D. Olson and A. Scahill (eds) *Lost and Othered Children in Contemporary Cinema*. Lanham: Lexington Books. 95-105.

Schickel, R. (1976) 'Bedeviled', *TIME Magazine*. Vol. 107, No. 27. 28 June. 46.

Schober, A. (2004) *Possessed Child Narratives in Literature and Film: Contrary States*. Houndmills, Basingstoke: Palgrave Macmillan.

Schock, P.A. (1993) '*The Marriage of Heaven and Hell*: Blake's Myth of Satan and its Cultural Matrix', *English Literary History*. Vol. 60, No. 2. 441-470.

Schreck, N. (2001) *The Satanic Screen: An Illustrated Guide to the Devil in Cinema*. London: Creation Books.

Schulman, B.J. and J.E. Zelizer (2008) 'Introduction', in B.J. Schulman and J.E. Zelizer (eds) *Rightward Bound: Making America Conservative in the 1970s*. Cambridge, MA; London: Harvard University Press. 1-10.

Screenwriter's Notebook – An Interview with Writer David Seltzer [short film] Director unknown. 20th Century Fox Entertainment, United States, 2006. [Special feature on *The Omen Collection: Deluxe Edition*, Blu-ray.]

Seltzer, D. (n.d.) 'How I wrote *The Omen* – One of the Scariest Movies of all Time', BBC Radio 4. Available at https://www.bbc.co.uk/programmes/articles/4hQKj3MfGfvR9sctTc dVn2d/how-i-wrote-the-omen-one-of-the-scariest-movies-of-all-time [accessed 21 May 2020]

Seltzer, D. (1975) *The Omen*. Original screenplay. Revised 8 September. Available at http://www.dailyscript.com/scripts/Omen.pdf [accessed 24 October 2021].

Seltzer, D. (1976) *The Omen*. London: Futura.

Shales, T. (1976) 'A Deadly Thriller', *Washington Post*. 26 June. C1+

Shay, D. (1976) 'Filming *The Omen*', *Cinefantastique*. Vol. 5, No. 3. 40-47.

Shay, D. (1978) 'Coming: *Damien – The Omen Part II*', Cinefantastique. Vol. 7, No. 1. 53-54.

Showalter, E. (1998) *Hystories: Hysterical Epidemics and Modern Culture*. London: Picador.

Simon, E. (2017) '"The One Who Knocks": Milton's Lucifer and the American Tragic Character', in G. Thuswaldner and D. Russ (eds) *The Hermeneutics of Hell: Visions and Representations of the Devil in World Literature*. New York: Palgrave Macmillan. 271-290.

Sophocles. (1984) *The Three Theban Plays: Antigone, Oedipus the King, Oedipus at Colonus*. Trans. Robert Fagles. New York: Penguin.

Stanford, Peter (1998) *The Devil: A Biography*. London: Arrow.

Sturm, T. (2012) 'Hal Lindsey's Geopolitical future: Towards a Cartographic Theory of Anticipatory Arrows', *Journal of Maps*. Vol. 7, No. 1. 39-45.

Sutton, M. (1981) Review of *The Final Conflict, Films and Filming*. Vol. 325. Oct. 45-46.

Sweetnam, M.S. (2011) 'Hal Lindsay [sic] and the Great Dispensational Mutation.' *Journal of Religion and Popular Culture*. Vol. 23, No. 2, available at Gale Academic OneFile, link.gale.com/apps/doc/A292993183/AONE?u=unimelb&sid=bookmarkAONE&xid=61b42539

Thomas, K. (1976) '*The Omen* a Scare Package', *Los Angeles Times*. 25 June. G1+

Thompson, H.S. (1994) 'He was a Crook', *The Atlantic*. July, available at https://www.theatlantic.com/magazine/archive/1994/07/he-was-a-crook/308699/[accessed 25 March 2021]. [Originally published in *Rolling Stone*, 16 June 1994.]

Thomson, D. (2016) *The New Biographical Dictionary of Film*. 6th ed. New York: Knopf.

Time Out. (2021) 'The 100 Best Horror Films of All Time.' 10 December. Available at https://www.timeout.com/film/best-horror-films [accessed 30 January 2022]

Todorov, T. (1975) *The Fantastic: A Structural Approach to a Literary Genre*. Ithaca, New York: Cornell University Press.

Travers, P. (2006) Review of *The Omen, Rolling Stone*. 8 June, available at https://www.rollingstone.com/movies/movie-reviews/the-omen-247836/ [accessed 13 June 2020].

Tudor, A. (1989) *Monsters and Mad Scientists: A Cultural History of the Horror Movie*. Oxford: Basil Blackwell.

Vachon, B. (1971) 'Witches are Rising', *Look*. Vol. 35, No. 17. 24 August. 40-44.

Ward, J.P. (1981) Review of *The Final Conflict, Films in Review*. Vol. 32. May. 312.

Wheen, F. (2007) *Strange Days Indeed: The Golden Age of Paranoia*. London: Fourth Estate, 2009.

Whitman, M. (1981) Review of *The Final Conflict, Films Illustrated*. Vol. 11. 5 October. 5.

Williams, R. (1989) *Resources of Hope: Culture, Democracy, Socialism*, ed. R. Gale and intro. by R. Blackburn. London and New York: Verso.

Williams, T. (2014) *Hearths of Darkness: The Family in the American Horror Film*. Updated ed. Jackson: University of Mississippi Press.

Wills, Garry (2000) *Reagan's America: Innocents at Home*. New York: Penguin.

Wood, R. (1976) 'Return of the Repressed', *The Times Literary Supplement*. 31 December. No. 3213. 12.

Wood, R. (2003) *Hollywood from Vietnam to Reagan ... and Beyond*. New York: Columbia University Press.

DEVIL'S ADVOCATES

"Auteur Publishing's new Devil's Advocates critiques on individual titles offer bracingly fresh perspectives from passionate writers. The series will perfectly complement the BFI archive volumes." Christopher Fowler, Independent on Sunday

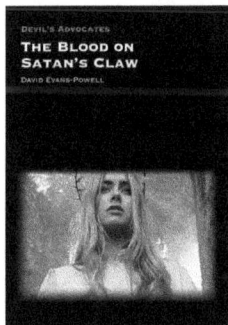

THE BLOOD ON SATAN'S CLAW – DAVID EVANS-POWELL

"Evans-Powell has written a powerful and fascinating monograph that is very readable. He manages to cram a lot of intriguing detail into such a short book yet it never feels as though the reader is overloaded with information, and it always feels relevant and interesting." – Folk Horror Revival

PREVENGE – ANDREW GRAVES

"Andrew Graves offers a suitably appreciative, perceptive celebration of a movie that never wanted to be pigeonholed for the sake of its commercial prospects... This concise, engaging DEVIL'S ADVOCATES monograph is... a witty, insightful read that will inspire you to revisit Lowe's glorious back catalogue." – FrightFest

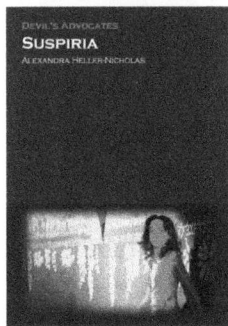

SUSPIRIA – ALEXANDRA HELLER-NICHOLAS

"This is a really sharp book, and an excellent series... Brief, compact and authoritative, these are the volumes to beat on these classic genre films." – Frame by Frame

www.ingramcontent.com/pod-product-compliance
Lightning Source LLC
Chambersburg PA
CBHW062347300326
41947CB00013B/1680